film
makers
on
film

LAURENCE KING

First published in Great Britain in 2021 by
Laurence King Publishing Ltd
Carmelite House
50 Victoria Embankment
London EC4Y 0DZ

An Hachette UK Company

1 3 5 7 9 10 8 6 4 2

Filmmakers on Film is based on an original concept
by Henry Carroll

A CIP catalogue record for this book
is available from the British Library.

ISBN: 978-0-85782-903-0

Design concept: Atelier Dyakova
Cover design: Mylène Mozas
Origination by F1 Colour, London
Printed in Malaysia by Vivar Sdn Bhd

Laurence King Publishing is committed
to ethical and sustainable production.
We are proud participants in
The Book Chain Project
bookchainproject.com®

www.laurenceking.com
www.orionbooks.co.uk

Cover: 'Little bathed in light', from the film
Moonlight directed by Barry Jenkins;
photo © 2015 David Bornfriend

ACKNOWLEDGEMENTS

Thanks to Henry Carroll, John Parton, Donald Dinwiddie,
Melissa Mellor, Maria Ranauro, Alex Coco, Florian Michelet,
and all at Laurence King and Hachette who ushered this
project forward and gave me the opportunity to write it
and the excuse to watch/re-watch a tonne of amazing
movies. Thanks to Ryan Swen, Mehelli Modi and Robert
Beeson for various handy research assists, and Mia,
Pedro, Isabel, Joe, Christine and Apichatpong for their
generous and insightful interviews. Thanks to my parents,
Ray and Ruth, for taking me to the cinema as a nipper
and leaving copies of *Time Out* and *Sight & Sound* around
the house, and all my colleagues at *Little White Lies* for
making sure I'm always up on the film chat. The majority
of my thanks, though, goes to my eternally understanding,
forgiving and empathetic wife Kayte and my darling
daughter Ivy for emotional support, covering my washing-
up duties, putting up with my organizational deficiencies
and getting me through those long, late nights.

– David Jenkins

DAVID JENKINS

film makers on film

How they create, craft & communicate

LAURENCE KING PUBLISHING

CONTENTS

INTRODUCTION

TO MAKE A GREAT FILM YOU HAVE TO BE A POET.

To make a great film you have to be a musician. To make a great film you have to be a photographer. To make a great film you have to be a novelist. To make a great film you have to be an actor. To make a great film you have to be a dancer. To make a great film you have to be a diarist. To make a great film you have to be an artist. To make a great film you have to be all of the above and more.

This book is a celebration of professional multi-hyphenates across the last century and a small fraction of the new one. These people are makers of montage, tellers of stories, composers of images – yet the mode, the means and the method all remain unique. Film's multifarious nature as a medium means it's rare that any two filmmakers will agree on its purpose. It can be used as a tool to serve a variety of functions, and there are filmmakers working today who strive to expand and diversify that list of functions.

I love the 50 filmmakers assembled here. Their inclusion is in no way intended as a canonical survey of the medium, but in fact hints at the possibility of a more expansive and liberated future canon (if, indeed, the very notion of 'the canon' has not outlived its cultural usefulness). In every chapter, I have tried simply to answer one question: what makes this filmmaker exceptional?

'A film is a petrified fountain of thought.'
Jean Cocteau

B: 1889 / **N:** French

Imagine the cinema screen as a pool of consciousness. Diving in offers the opportunity to explore exotic interior worlds; worlds that allow you to see yourself with a dreamlike clarity. The creative and flamboyant French maestro Jean Cocteau routinely made films featuring a reflective portal that allows a character to self-analyse (1930's *Le Sang d'un poète*), to fantasize over an erotic obsession (1946's *La Belle et la Bête*) or to rescue a departed lover from her underworld Bastille (1950's *Orphée*). More than half a century later, Cocteau's ineffably romantic films feel fresh and energized because he refused to hide his workings. His films allow us to inspect his hand-tooled innovations and see them for what they are. He demystifies the filmmaking process while leaving eccentric pockmarks of humane intent dashed across the celluloid. Water is the element that most readily applies to Cocteau, his indelible images trickling like a stream from one to the next, connected through symbols, framings, colours, contradictions and, sometimes, off-the-cuff camera tricks. This image from *La Belle et la Bête* sees Cocteau muse and lover Jean Marais as the Beast, carrying his beloved Belle along a corridor of candelabras that are mounted on human hands. The hybrid nature of his work bleeds out from theme and story into form and character. Everyday objects are retooled as the stuff of fantasia – it's an art and craft form of image-making that showcases the counterintuitive thought processes of creator, while also saying to the viewer: 'Yes, you can.'

La Belle et la Bête, 1946

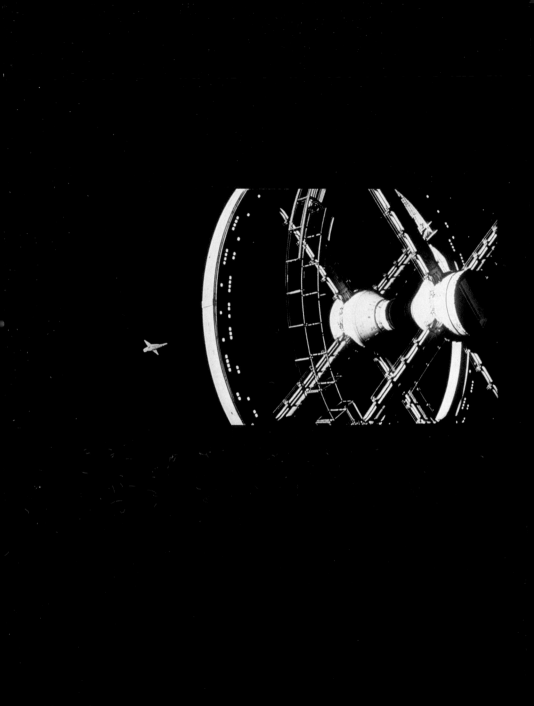

2001: A Space Odyssey, 1966

'... the basic purpose of a film ... [is] one of illumination, of showing the viewer something he can't see any other way.'

Stanley Kubrick

B: 1928 / **N:** American

A severe strain of rigour runs through the work of ultra-scrupulous photographer-turned-filmmaker Stanley Kubrick. His yen for innovation and exactitude resulted in the awe-inspiring special effect set pieces of 1968's *2001: A Space Odyssey*, in which a cosmic ballet plays out in the vortex of space. In Kubrick's hands, the camera becomes a wily, back-alley guide who is willing and able to show us hidden beauty and unseen decrepitude. He coined the ghostly aspect that came from the svelte camera movements achieved through snaking Steadicam shots in 1980's *The Shining*. His decision to have cinematographer John Alcott light interiors using candles in 1975's period epic *Barry Lyndon* gives the impression of a chiaroscuro Romantic-era canvas come to life. His subject matter, too, sought to peer behind the curtain of various private social enclaves, such as gangsters (*The Killing*, 1956), juvenile delinquents (*A Clockwork Orange*, 1971), marines in training (*Full Metal Jacket*, 1987), and the masked members of an elite New York sex cult (*Eyes Wide Shut*, 1999). While pretenders to Kubrick's throne scamper in the aisles – names such as Christopher Nolan or David Fincher come to mind – a debate still rages as to whether this vaunted director was a maker of pristine cinematic contraptions to be admired, rather than messy, humanist sagas to be cherished. There's an irony to the fact that the computerized space navigator HAL-9000 malfunctions in *2001: A Space Odyssey*, a film made by a technician who strove for astringent perfection at every turn.

'A film that can be described in words is not really a film.'
Michelangelo Antonioni

B: 1912 / **N:** Italian

Martin Scorsese talks about cinema as being a matter of what is in and out of the frame. For the Italian existentialist Michelangelo Antonioni, it's also a matter of what is in and out of the story. He was a filmmaker fascinated by absence rather than what Scorsese is referring to, which is negative space. His ironically titled 1960 film *L'Avventura* (The Adventure) traces the aftermath of a boat trip where one member of a small party disappears. The missing woman's boyfriend and best friend decide to scour the country for her. Antonioni monitors how this unseen figure inexorably impacts the relationship of the searchers. The notion of time and geography creating a remove from the reality of a tragic event – and naturally assuaging our sense of guilt – is one reading of this complex film. Their love affair is framed as being less than idyllic, suggesting something darker about our ability to love even when our lives are rife with ambient anxieties. This image is from the director's 1970 film *Zabriskie Point*, which imagines a utopian world in which capitalism itself – momentarily – becomes an absence. The perfect entry point for those looking to discover Antonioni is 1962's *L'Eclisse* (The Eclipse), in which, during its climactic sequence (beloved of Scorsese), narrative itself becomes the absence, as this film about the courtship of a beautiful Italian couple drifts into nothingness. With its protagonists departed on their own paths, the camera has literally nothing to look at. It is the ultimate movie fade-out.

Zabriskie Point, 1970

The Headless Woman, 2008

'A film for me is a mechanism to show thought, but I interpret thought as a mix of perception and emotion.'

Lucrecia Martel

B: 1966 / **N:** Argentinian

The actress in this image is María Onetto, star of Lucrecia Martel's 2008 film *The Headless Woman*. Her sideways glance does not allow us to see the expression on her face. It's almost as if she doesn't know which way to look, or she is averting the gaze of someone else. Onetto plays Vero, a bourgeois housewife who, while driving along a country road, glances down at her mobile phone momentarily and feels something roll underneath her tyres. Convincing herself it's a dog, she carries on with the trivialities of family life. Yet the uncertainty of this moment – of why she rejected the impulse to find out exactly what happened, an impulse perhaps born of societal duty – weighs heavily on her. Aspects of her life unravel. The incident is illustrative of a moment of realization and possible regret. The film offers a moral quandary, but also places us there on the path of warped perception. Could this all just be a nightmare? Martel's four feature films all zero in on protagonists who are largely blind to the world in which they are cocooned – suffering, exploitation, political corruption, religious zealotry, you name it.
From the elegantly slumming middle-class wastrels in 2001's *The Swamp*, to a preening eighteenth-century government administrator desperate to save his own hide in 2018's *Zama*, Martel's films are woozy, quixotic and disorientating. She lures us into a sensibility of experimentation, but ends up articulating her thesis of innate human selfishness with daunting clarity.

'No art passes our conscience in the way film does, and goes directly to our feelings, deep down into the dark rooms of our souls.'

Ingmar Bergman

B: 1918 / **N:** Swedish

There's a sequence in Ingmar Bergman's 1961 feature *Through a Glass Darkly* in which two characters converse on a boat out at sea. One, played by Max von Sydow, begins to berate the other, played by Gunnar Björnstrand: 'You're void of all feeling. You lack common decency. You're a craven coward.' Instead of expressing shock or upset, Björnstrand remains blank-faced in stoic acceptance of deficiencies he clearly believes to be true. Bergman's cinema is of a variety that cuts through the need for performative expressions of displeasure. When his actors do break loose, it's usually for reasons of more sustained or extreme debasement, the result of a visit to that dark room of the soul. Many of Bergman's most famous works depict people suffering while an apathetic God watches over them, and films such as *The Silence* (1963) and *The Seventh Seal* (1957) even attempt to explain our need for spiritual consolation in an unforgiving world. While Bergman made many challenging, intense films, 1966's *Persona* is perhaps the one that has everything. It is a mysterious, inscrutable object involving a mute actor and her caregiver, and a storyline that playfully transcends binary interpretation. As his two leads, played by Bibi Andersson and Liv Ullmann, attempt to decipher the motivations of the other during a period of convalescence on a remote island, Bergman constantly alters the rules of the game, allowing the viewer to take nothing for granted, and to drink in this intoxicating film as a potion of pure feeling.

Persona, 1966

Five Dedicated to Ozu, 2003

'In my mind, our dreams are windows in our lives, and the significance of cinema is in its similarity to these windows.'

Abbas Kiarostami

B: 1940 / **N:** Iranian

The windows referenced by Iranian director Abbas Kiarostami feature time and again in his films. They offer a vision of internal lives often troubled by external pressures – pressures that range from the political to the theatrical and the public to the private. They sometimes allow a character to see the world anew, such as at the end of his lugubriously enigmatic 2010 film *Certified Copy*. They also place poetic emphasis on the quotidian, such as the ten intimate vignettes filmed from the dashboard of a car in his 2002 film *Ten*. Kiarostami started out as a maker of educational films for children, which often revolved around a simple moral conundrum. The dreamlike effect of the camera, and its ability to complicate an image through subtle stresses and expressive framing, allowed the director to take this simplicity to a new level. He pared back his style to the point of abstraction, but achieved this by refracting stories through windows piled up on top of one another. His 2003 film *Five Dedicated to Ozu* – comprising five long takes, all around 16 minutes in length – features a sequence in which a flock of ducks scampers past the camera from left to right. Following a brief pause, the ducks then run back in the opposite direction. Why? Is someone off camera directing the ducks? Is it ever possible to truly believe and accept the images we see on a screen, or must we always acknowledge that dreamlike remove?

'My instinct is that it all comes down to meaning, and you return to films where there's some sort of tight emotional rationale.'

Jane Campion

B: 1954 / **N:** New Zealander

This quotation could refer directly to Jane Campion's multi-award-winning 1993 feature *The Piano*, in which Holly Hunter's mute waif conducts a series of erotic relationships with her husband, another man, her daughter and the instrument referenced in the film's title. The power of *The Piano* derives from the way the writer–director minutely calibrates (and differentiates) the emotional tenor of each relationship: through framing and performance, and also by ushering the dramatic contours of the landscape – a sodden beachside settlement in nineteenth-century New Zealand – into the heart of her tragic heroine. Indeed, bodies and landscapes are one and the same in this film: both are to be explored, sometimes with tenderness, sometimes with brutality. Campion has long been interested in cautious, reticent women and how they navigate a terrain of suppressed sexual longing, interpersonal dysfunction, artistic fulfilment and professional fortitude. Her 1990 masterpiece *An Angel at My Table* chronicles the formative years of poet and author Janet Frame, rejecting a conventional narrative arc in favour of presenting life as a meandering stream of confusion and indignity. Meanwhile, 2009's *Bright Star* details an intense love affair between the Romantic poet John Keats and his neighbour Fanny Brawne that withers before it has a chance to fully blossom. The relationship is scuppered – as it so often is – by the fragility of the human body. Campion's films are notable for their rhapsodic artistry, as well as for the centring of female desire that, in its intensity, traverses the full spectrum of emotions.

The Piano, 1993

Uncle Boonmee Who Can Recall
His Past Lives, 2010

'Each film has its own language – the movie tells you how it wants to be told.'

Apichatpong Weerasethakul

B: 1970 / **N:** Thai

Many of the subjects of this volume have been selected because of their willingness to reject conventional wisdom apropos the size, shape and scope of traditional motion pictures. Apichatpong Weerasethakul makes films that draw on a multiplicity of creative sources, though the main reason they seldom have a beginning, middle and end is that he considers time to be a fluid construct. Cinema is merely a portal into realms that remain teasingly inaccessible to us in our day-to-day lives, but that can be unlocked via a mix of imagination and knowledge. He sees the present as the product of our national myths and histories, and he posits that we're living with the constant presence of spectres – from the past, the future and from a place beyond comprehension. His 2010 Palme d'Or-winning *Uncle Boonmee Who Can Recall His Past Lives* offers the most user-friendly distillation of his softly spoken vision, bringing together scenes of catfish cunnilingus and monkey ghosts with eloquent depictions of social realist normalcy, as people and ghosts wrestle with their place on Earth and in time. If this all sounds maddeningly complex, that couldn't be further from the truth: where Apichatpong's work may require a little getting used to, his ability to capture the raw poetry of the everyday is second to none. Just watch the final scene of *Syndromes and a Century* (2006), in which a group of people exercise together in a public park, and try to name a more perfect celluloid vision of pure happiness.

APICHATPONG WEERASETHAKUL

'Dreaming has become part of a working process.'

Syndromes and a Century, 2006

When did you first become aware of this notion of human perception existing over multiple planes – a notion that plays such an important role in your films?

I think growing up in Thailand, with its mixture of Buddhism, Hinduism and animism, contributed to my belief that there is coexistence and transmutation between physical beings (humans, animals, plants) and invisible beings (gods and ghosts). Even though I try to shake the idea off, I cannot totally get rid of it. When I see a tree, I assume there is a spirit in it, and that later it will move somewhere else. I am temporarily in this body, and when my heart stops, I will move somewhere else.

How much does the content of your dreams feed your creativity during your waking life?

I keep a dream journal whenever I can. I am curious about the logic (non-logic) in dreams. When I work on something, sometimes a revelation appears in a dream. So dreaming has become part of a working process.

How do you document your ideas as they come to you on a day-by-day basis? How do you choose which ones are worth developing further?

I jot down ideas and situations in my notebooks, and lately into my phone or computer. Mostly they are mundane things. Sometimes they are just words or images that I photograph or sketch. Certain things will keep reappearing or connecting with one another.

**You've talked about how you are initially
drawn to locations when thinking about
ideas for films. The light is important to you.
What are the different types of light, and
which do you like best?**

I like obscured lights. Lights with shadows
or lights at night. Or the absence of light.
They trigger imagination and, sometimes, fear.
I was attracted to American B horror movies in
the VHS days which had minimal lighting.

**When you have developed a connection
to a location, when do thoughts of framing
or scene choreography come in?**

I often mix and match situations and locations.
Or reconstruct something from childhood
memory. I prefer long shots, so we often set
up an open set. Then I do a preliminary block
shot, and afterwards, finalize the framing with
the DoP [director of photography].

**The way you use still images in your films
is very striking and moving. They evoke
nostalgia, history and private memory.
Do you remember when and why you decided
to introduce these 'slide shows' into films?**

Do I use the stills often? I only remember
using it in *Boonmee* [*Uncle Boonmee Who
Can Recall His Past Lives*, 2010], and a bit
in *Tropical Malady* (2004). Mostly those
particular scenes involve a reference to the
illusory nature of time. In *Tropical Malady*
it was in the script, but in *Boonmee* it
probably came during the editing.
They were the points when the film shifted
perspectives, spaces, revealing the
documentation process... that made the
film ignore its mission to lull the audience
with its linear flow of time. I didn't intend
to make a statement but I felt it was natural.
It reflected the characters' journey at
that point.

One of my favourite scenes in your films is the final sequence set in the park in *Syndromes and a Century* (2006), as it offers something I never see in cinema: a vision of happiness. When it comes to people – and maybe Thai people – do you feel that happiness is our human default?

I'm not sure of our default mode. I guess when you are aware of the pure movements, colours, without analysing (the film) – as it appeared in that last scene – you operate as if you are meditating. You detach yourself from the narrative and are liberated. I had this sensation when I watched experimental films, for example. To me it is not necessarily happiness but neutral peace.

APICHATPONG WEERASETHAKUL
Thai director known for his uniquely ethereal film and gallery work. Tim Burton's jury awarded his film *Uncle Boonmee Who Can Recall His Past Lives* the Palme d'Or at the 2010 Cannes Film Festival. Between making features – such as 2004's *Tropical Malady*, 2006's *Syndromes and a Century* and 2015's *Cemetery of Splendour* – he has also made numerous shorts and installations for festivals and arts bodies across the globe. His 2021 film *Memoria* is his first to employ a Hollywood star (Tilda Swinton), and it won the Jury Prize at the 2021 Cannes Film Festival.

Blue Velvet, 1986

'Film can't just be a long line of bliss. There's something we all like about the human struggle.'

David Lynch

B: 1946 / N: American

To source ideas and images for his films, David Lynch plunges into the pool of his subconscious via transcendental meditation. What makes his work so exceptional – and idiosyncratic – is a willingness to share the fruits of these interior deep dives and make sure they are largely unadorned and uncensored. It is the life of the mind writ large, and it has meant that, as a modern behemoth of cinematic creativity, Lynch has been able to perch in that liminal space between traditional romantic genre cinema and full-bore experimentation that sometimes borders on the abstract. One moment that remains emblematic of his project is the breathtaking opening sequence to 1986's *Blue Velvet*, in which a hauntingly manicured vision of provincial America is punctured with scenes of a man suffering a stroke while spraying his lawn, followed by a delve into the grass, where we experience the sub-aural thrum of an ants' nest. We run the gamut between ethereal beauty and nauseating dread in record time. In the mellow pageant of American life, Lynch sees beauty and horror not so much as opposite sides of the same coin, but as a singular entity that can permeate everyone and everything simultaneously. His formidable 1977 debut *Eraserhead* looked at birthing and parenthood through a surreally baroque lens, while later works, such as *Wild at Heart* (1990) and *Twin Peaks: Fire Walk with Me* (1992), danced on the precipice where raging, intense love tips over into splenetic violence.

'As long as movies are depressing, life isn't.'

Rainer Werner Fassbinder

B: 1945 / **N:** German

There is no better way to encapsulate the modus operandi of German filmmaker Rainer Werner Fassbinder than to quote the title of his 1969 debut feature: *Love Is Colder than Death*. Whether it's an obsession or a drawn-out lamentation, Fassbinder's body of work – with a few minor exceptions – offers variations on the observation that human beings are simply not compatible with one another, and that love is merely a social construct or a cheap illusion helping to pass the time or contrive social order. He rarely celebrates individualism too, viewing it as either a road to ruin (see *The Marriage of Maria Braun*, 1979) or a nexus of eternal loneliness (*Veronika Voss*, 1982; *Fox and His Friends*, 1975). And yet for someone who deals primarily in shades of human alienation, his films are rapturous, heartbreaking, cynical and tragically perspicuous. A cinematic communicator par excellence, Fassbinder employed style entirely at the service of his bitter material, most often opting for direct, terse compositions, and relying on members of his regular acting company to do the emotional heavy lifting. *The Bitter Tears of Petra Von Kant* (1972) displays his aptitude for turning limitation into leverage as he tells of an arrogant celebrity fashion designer learning that she can't have everything she wants in this world, all set within the confines of a small, stifling and impeccably decorated apartment. Much poisonous verbiage flows from the screen, but the film says more about love's crooked disposition than most artists manage in a lifetime.

The Bitter Tears of Petra Von Kant, 1972

'Always make the audience suffer as much as possible.'

Alfred Hitchcock

B: 1899 / **N:** British

Show the bomb. Show the audience the fuse – and just how far away it is. Light the fuse. Alfred Hitchcock did not earn the sobriquet of 'master of suspense' for nothing, and his films demonstrate an almost algorithmic understanding of how to create images that will transport the derrière of a viewer to the edge of its seat. But there's more to Hitchcock than thermodynamics and clinical methodology. He made his fair share of vivacious entertainments, such as the sun-bleached cat burglar antics of *To Catch a Thief* (1955), or the wisecracking chase comedy *North by Northwest* (1959). Yet his greatest works combine a ruthless technical prowess with outré subject matter. *Vertigo* (1958) is a self-reflexive, psychoanalytic film noir about the line between obsession and perversion, and how that mindset naturally relates to the toil of an artist. In *Rear Window* (1954) he presents the very act of watching the film as like being trapped by circumstance in an unfolding drama. Two films about murderers can be chalked up as his most disturbing: *Frenzy* (1972), which goes to great lengths to deglamorize the activities of a gentleman serial killer; and 1960's *Psycho*, which not only dispatches its lead character ahead of time, but then rips away the comfort blanket of a cosy, three-act structure. The shower scene, in which a shadowy figure stabs Janet Leigh in time to Bernard Herrmann's staccato violin screeches, is counted among the greatest moments in the medium.

'I have no desire to cuddle my audience.'

Věra Chytilová

B: 1929 / **N:** Czech

The brilliant Czech filmmaker Věra Chytilová wore the description 'abrasiveness' as a stylistic badge of honour, and she addressed her audience in a thrillingly confrontational manner. Take, for example, her 1979 film *Panelstory*, which seeks to recreate the experience of life in a hideous Soviet housing conurbation, with camerawork that teeters just on the right side of the queasily voyeuristic, and shrill sound design that makes you want to bury your head in a pillow. And yet she taps into essential truths about the dynamics of community and the irritating aspect of close-quarters living. The film she is best known for, however, is 1966's *Daisies*, a non-narrative exploration into rebellion and political anarchism in which two young women casually reject the timeworn precepts of feminine politesse, and proceed blithely to destroy everything and everyone around them. Even though Chytilová worked with symbolism and allegory to articulate her strident political convictions, she was blackballed from making films in communist Czechoslovakia for perceived seditious activity, and she often found it hard to keep working. Yet this seam of abrasiveness is cut through with sincere passion and a tremendous eye for striking juxtapositions – both visual and thematic. Her outrageous revenge film *Traps* (1998) sets its male-genital-slashing agenda with scenes of piglets being neutered, while her more wistful and reflective debut feature, *Something Different* (1963), sets duelling tales of a modern ballet dancer and a harried housewife side by side to present the crushing toils of womanhood.

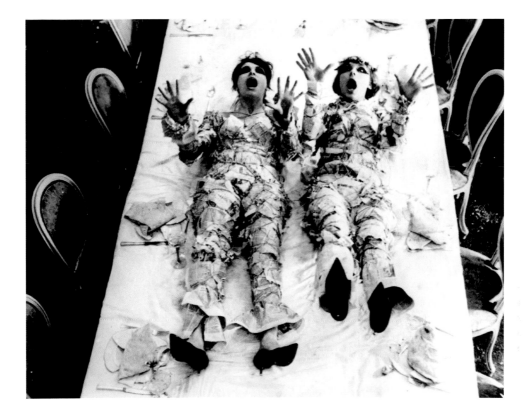

Daisies, 1966

The Big City, 1963

'I don't begin by formulating a moral attitude and then making a film.'

Satyajit Ray

B: 1921 / **N:** Indian

There's a procedural aspect to the films of Indian writer–director Satyajit Ray. To generalize, he adopts a simple social quandary, sits at a cautious remove and observes as it plays out. His films, often loaded with symbolism, demonstrate an abiding interest in uncovering the cultural mores that hamper social and political progress in India. His global renown stems largely from his lyrical 1955 debut feature, *Pather Panchali*, which unsparingly charts the lives of a dirt-poor family in rural Bengal. The film accrues its power through Ray's attempt to place the viewer at the scene, to entrench the story in the sights and sounds of this crumbling, weather-beaten enclave barely fit for human habitation. Another formative masterpiece is 1958's *The Music Room*, which asks the viewer to empathize with an aristocrat and landlord as he watches his fiefdom come to ruin while he indulges his pleasure of listening to music. Again, Ray enhances this material by shifting it away from political point-scoring, trying instead to understand what makes a man choose the precipitous path of self-annihilation. Two of his greatest films are about women questioning their second-tier status in modern India: *The Big City* (1963), about a housewife defying the wishes of her husband by moving into the world of work; and 1964's *Charulata*, in which the wife of a press baron fulfils her literary and romantic aspirations in the shadows. Among other things, Ray was a master of composing for the (square) Academy ratio.

'Cinema is like an ongoing political rally with the audience. In a movie theatre, you have Catholics, Muslims, Gaullists, Communists if the film is good.'

Ousmane Sembène

B: 1923 / **N:** Senegalese

The novelist, activist and filmmaker Ousmane Sembène is considered the first Black African to have made a film in Africa, namely his evocative and angry 1963 short *The Wagoner*. Yet the revolutionary aspect of his nascent career behind the camera also served as the ideological marrow of his filmed output over the next half-century, right up until his outspoken and engrossing polemic against female circumcision, 2004's *Moolaadé*. His most famous films tend to focus on abuses meted out against the working class and prod at the still-weeping scars of colonial endeavour in Africa. It's a stall he set out with ruthless efficiency in 1966's harrowing *Black Girl*, about a young peasant from Dakar who is plucked from a crowd by haughty white French slave tourists and invited to work as a housemaid in their chic Parisian abode. She accepts the offer, and is ritually abused and humiliated in her new role. One of Sembène's funniest films is 1975's anarchic political comedy *Xala*, in which a vainglorious politician (working as a puppet for white colonial oppressors) is cursed with impotency when he decides to take a third wife, and then shirks his professional duties in an attempt to break the spell. The situation becomes symbolic of the impulses that bring about chronic political corruption, where feathering the personal nest is always preferable to the noble grind of public service. But Sembène's candid sideswipes are always rooted in the specific tragedies that occurred on African soil.

Xala, 1975

Ivan's Childhood, 1962

'What is the essence of the director's work? We could define it as sculpting in time.'

Andrei Tarkovsky

B: 1932 / **N:** Russian

Russian maestro Andrei Tarkovsky made films about why life is worth living and why death is worth dying. He took up the mantle of locating meaning in the evanescence of existence, whether through confirming the presence of an obscure, spiritual higher power (1966's *Andrei Rublev*), speculating on our complex relationship with the untapped cosmos (1972's *Solaris*), or merely reflecting (as in 1979's *Stalker*) our collective desire to find a secret place of infinite knowledge and understanding that will allow us to answer the one true question: why? In his later films, he shifted away from contemplating matters metaphysical to focus on stories that emulate human memory and our perception of time (1975's *Mirror* and 1983's *Nostalgia*). In his 1985 book *Sculpting in Time*, he drilled down into his creative impulses and waxed philosophical about the power of the camera as a piece of heavy machinery that can be used to make art through minutely calibrated (and intellectually invested) montage and framing. All his later inspirational and aesthetically dazzling achievements were foreshadowed in his 1962 debut proper, *Ivan's Childhood*, a deceptively conventional drama about a 12-year-old boy acting as a messenger on the Russian front during World War II. From its opening dream sequence onwards, Tarkovsky daintily chips away at time with his trusty arsenal of tools, obsessed by the fragility of human consciousness in a world rife with torments and reasons to lose faith in it all.

'We don't like displays of acting.'
Christine Molloy & Joe Lawlor

B: 1963 and 1965 / **N:** Irish

The time-honoured sequence shot has taken something of a battering in recent times, as it has become seen as a form of cinematic voguing – of technical showmanship for its own sake. Yet consider the early short work of Irish filmmakers Christine Molloy and Joe Lawlor (aka Desperate Optimists), titles such as 2004's *Who Killed Brown Owl?* or 2005's *Leisure Centre* (both of which are shot in a single take), and this swaggering mode is shown in a humble and empathetic light, employed to express the humour, pain and joyful thrum of communal civic life. The pair graduated to film via experimental theatre, and their idiosyncratic work, which is often made on a threadbare budget, brims with conceptual boldness and a sincere love (and keen understanding) of mid-century European arthouse cinema. The masterful *Helen* (2008) tips its hat to Italian maestro Michelangelo Antonioni in telling of a young woman hired to recreate the final moments of her missing classmate for a television appeal. Helen, the actor, ends up using this opportunity to analyse her own deprived upbringing, and the film goes on to pose tough questions about alienation and individuality. Their ensuing feature work comprises a catalogue of human disconnection: 2013's *Mister John* sees a man attempt to tie up the loose ends of his estranged dead brother, only to discover just how estranged he actually was; 2016's puckish documentary *Further Beyond* makes the case for impressionism and poetry in the movie biopic; and 2019's *Rose Plays Julie* sees an orphaned woman heading down the dark rabbit hole of her natural parentage, only to discover abject horror.

Helen, 2008

CHRISTINE MOLLOY
& JOE LAWLOR

'Filming is about re-finding the clarity that you had when you were writing.'

Rose Plays Julie, 2019

Since you've been making films, what has changed the most for you when it comes to your process?

Christine: The writing process is the thing that's changed the most. You always have to start with a script, which is not the way we worked when we made theatre, as we would write the script last. And with *Helen* [2008] we kind of wrote the script last also. We did a lot of work similar to the things we'd done in theatre, albeit at a location rather than on a stage. We built up the performers we wanted to work with, who are all non-actors, and thought about where we wanted to film and what we wanted to film. And it was all under our control because it was an art project. We didn't have to jump through the [industry] hoops. We actually knew very little about what it meant to make a feature film. That part of it was learned on the job, which can be quite exposing, especially when you're in the filming part of it. I wasn't even sure what a first AD [assistant director] was. We kinda knew by the time we'd put our crew together. And *Helen* was very interesting because it's very much an art project made up of these long takes, so it's about doing two shots a day. You can learn a lot if everything's slowed down and you're working on film. There are two big set-ups – they feel more like theatre because they take place over time. You focus a lot on the choreography of the camera. But we probably came out of *Helen* without knowing a huge amount about making film in the more conventional way, where you start with a script. Working on *Mister John* [2013] that was a huge learning process.

What is the first thing you do when embarking on a new project?

Christine: We start a film by talking a lot. We walk and talk … when we're in that early development stage and trying to figure out what the idea is and what's at the heart of it. And also how it'll chime with our ongoing interests in identity, which is a theme that's been woven through all our work. I would say that, even with *Mister John*, we didn't really understand how the writing process worked.

Joe: And that's not necessarily a bad thing. Crews know what they're doing because they're doing it every day. The DoP [director of photography] that we worked regularly with, Ole [Bratt Birkeland], would say that often the most inexperienced person on the set is the director. Which is true, but as we would point out to Ole (or any other DoP), as writers and directors we're the only ones who have thought about this specific film all day long for years, and that's the only thing that really matters at the end of the day. So [the DoP's] contribution, or anyone else's for that matter, is only ever worth a fraction of ours. Equally, someone's technical proficiency (which is critical by the way) is worth jack shit when compared to the filmmaker's insight into the narrative structure and character psychology and, critically, how the filmmaker wants the end film to be formally expressed.

Do you ever find yourself working to the dictates of the film industry?

Joe: Oh, we have no idea what the film industry wants. … And we also don't give a shit. We like film, we like going to the cinema, so that's our relationship with the industry. In terms of writing a treatment, it's about understanding the value of architecture. A screenplay is not a literary form, it's an architectural form. The more you understand that blueprint, the more complete and robust that screenplay will be.

Christine: You can never untangle [a film] from the way things are funded. We've had funding for development, and the money … is very low. It's also given out in dribs and drabs [because] it's contractual, so you'll get a certain amount of money when you sign, then the next amount on the first draft, and the next on delivery. That has pulled us away from the treatment really quickly, because unless we get cracking on a draft, we're not getting paid. We've done a couple of things on spec in the lockdown because we've failed to get funding for them, which means we're not under the same pressure to start on a draft when we're not even ready to do that. This is a personal thing. We're not advocating this to other people. Treatments are documents that are used to get development money. They're usually 15 pages, but the ones we have are about 30 pages.

Joe: Tempo is a really important thing, along with architecture. The rhythm of how you write. We used to believe we were slow writers. It turns out we're pretty quick – if you allow us to write! So the only people who allow that are ourselves. For *Helen*, the creative process was entirely down to us, as it was about reaching out to communities and working with people. We controlled that rhythm. If you're going down a different road, ideally you'll end up with a different film, as opposed to a beginning, middle and end. We have applied to production funds, who have people called external readers, and they will do readings of your script, approaching it in a very beginning, middle and end way. 'Character didn't do this by page 30, which is the first third, and they really should have.' Are you kidding me? It's amazing how much conventional thinking there is out there.

Christine: In terms of collaborating, we talk a lot, we write treatments together, but when it comes to writing a script, after all the prep work, Joe will always do the first draft. Always. And that's about understanding after all these years what our strengths are. And who's not afraid of the blank piece of

paper. But by the point that we're looking at the blank piece of paper, we've already done a lot of work. And then, once that's there, it just goes back and forth until we arrive at the point where we're ready to give it over to somebody. The writing is a specific journey in terms of our collaboration. We work together but that doesn't mean we're the same and that we have the same strengths. When it comes to directing it's very different because we've got to work together. On a set, there's not very much that would be different for anyone except for the fact that there's two of us.

Because you're so aligned in the pre-production stage, does that mean that the shoot is a little easier as you both have a very strong idea of what it is you want to do?

Christine: When people ask questions, we generally know the answers, but it's a place that can throw a lot of curveballs. All the films we've made are low budget, so the time we have with the camera is pretty limited, [which makes it] a very intense environment.

Joe: I do recall there was a moment when we were filming *Rose Plays Julie* and I was talking to Ann Skelly, who plays the lead part. We were going to do a scene that was a waking dream she had about her and her father. She comes up and says, 'I was thinking about it last night, should I wear the wig for this scene or not?' And I just didn't have the answer to that question. … About a year ago I did have the answer, but at that moment I didn't … Of course, she needed to know now. So Christine was there to answer that question. You can go through a thinking process and forget what you thought about. Filming is about re-finding the clarity that you had when you were writing. When you're directing, it's much more like a field of battle. There isn't a lot of room for thinking. You're always surprised because actors in particular – especially smart ones like Ann – tend to ask actor questions. And we don't necessarily ask actor questions. We'll ask audience questions. We'll ask writer questions and director questions. But actors have a very particular way of working and they'll ask a very unpredictable set of questions about characters.

Christine: We spent a lot of time in our script for *Rose Plays Julie* describing the archaeological dig site, which had to be all mucky and earthy and wet and soggy. We needed to find the right field and hill fairly close to our unit base because in Ireland there's a very particular set of restrictions that we only heard about when we actually rocked into pre-production, to do with where you can film. You have your unit base, then you've got a 16-mile radius around that where you can film. And that's it. And if you film outside that circle, you incur huge penalties, and if you're on a small budget, you ain't gonna go outside, so you've got to find your field and your hill inside [it]. Our unit base was near the coast, so most of our radius contained water and not land. So one day in pre-production you find yourself on the side of a hill in Wicklow (nicely inside the radius) staring into a massive hole in the ground which isn't mucky at all. It's chalky and dry, and looks more like something you'd find in the Atlas Mountains, rather than rain-sodden Ireland. And this changes things because you can't now film the scene the way you'd written it. Instead you have to start reimagining it. Thinking about it in a new way. And you convince yourself you never really wanted a mucky field in the first place. And that's not far from the truth because it was only ever just an idea that you clung to, to get you this far. There's an awful lot of 're-thinking' that goes on in that short space of time.

Joe: Don't get too wedded to your script because you may have overrun in the morning. You have lunch. Then you realize, that complex scene for the afternoon, you now have an hour and a half to shoot it. And you've got to do some very quick calibrating. If someone is inexperienced, they might want to hang on to a particular shot and they might want to get it right before they move on. But now you've lost a lot of time. And that leads you to compromise later shots. Or shots get dropped, so you have fewer options for editing. Or maybe you can't even complete your story because you've missed a chunk. There's that great comment that's been going around for years: 'Hollywood in the morning, Hollyoaks in the afternoon.' And it's absolutely true.

CHRISTINE MOLLOY & JOE LAWLOR
Known as Desperate Optimists, Irish duo Molloy and Lawlor gravitated to film via theatre and community art, and the spirit of that formative career imbues their later screen work. Their run started with a collection of celebrated shorts that sat under the thematic banner of Civic Life, and 2008's *Helen* marks their shift into feature-making and their interest in notions of identity. *Mister John* (2013) saw them decamping to Singapore, while *Further Beyond* (2016) marks their first foray into the documentary essay field. Their most recent film is *Rose Plays Julie* (2019), about an adoptee who tries to trace her birth parents.

'Film is not analysis, it is the agitation of mind; cinema comes from the country fair and the circus, not from art and academicism.'

Werner Herzog

B: 1942 / **N:** German

There's a quaint saying that claims a journey is less about the destination than it is about the friends we make along the way. Werner Herzog believes not only that the very concept of a destination is a fallacy, but that 'friends' are in fact the embodiment of evil and terror. Watch 'bad trip' movies such as *The Enigma of Kaspar Hauser* (1974), *Aguirre, Wrath of God* (1977) or *Fitzcarraldo* (1982), and it's clear that Herzog's apparent cynicism is articulated with such wry levity and eccentricity as to make those films seem surprisingly affirmative and, perhaps, even ecstatic. This may be because, as a visual storyteller, Herzog is driven by primal images that speak for themselves and are shorn of unnecessary intellectualizing. Think of the blazing oil fields resembling an Old Testament vision of hell on Earth in 1992's *Lessons of Darkness*; the slo-mo shots of a ski jumper hanging between life and death in 1974's *The Great Ecstasy of Woodcarver Steiner*; or the chicken that dances for coins while the hero of 1977's *Stroszek* blows his brains out on a chairlift. In his documentary work, the director has made a name for himself with his playful commentaries on the artists of prehistory (2010's *Cave of Forgotten Dreams*) or the incomprehensible suicidal impulse of a lost Antarctic penguin (2007's *Encounters at the End of the World*). He believes that cinema is about preserving – and sometimes inventing – mysteries rather than solving them.

Fitzcarraldo, 1992

The Virgin Suicides, 1999

'Making films is like making stuff together as kids.'

Sofia Coppola

B: 1971 / **N:** American

Early on in her career, Sofia Coppola made films that were like shadow-tinted daydreams. With their gauzy aesthetics and ambient soundtracks, her work captured the lives of a number of girls and women who all stood at vital junctures on the road to romantic maturation. Her films often capture a time filled with wonderment and delight, but there's always a perfume of melancholy hanging in the air as the clock ticks away and the momentary joy fades with it. Swiftly, the system in which these characters operate closes in and extinguishes these waking reveries. The causes range from fundamentalist religion (1999's *The Virgin Suicides*) to the stifling strictures of marriage (2003's *Lost in Translation*), and even the oppressive customs of the Ancien Régime (2006's *Marie Antoinette*). What makes her films so impactful – and so moving – is that she leans on the notion of carefree fun as a way to build characters and present aspects of life that so rarely find their way onto screen. In 2013's underrated *The Bling Ring*, she adapted the ripped-from-the-headlines tale of a gang of chancer teens who stole trinkets from super-rich celebrities knowing they wouldn't be missed.
It channels the satirical intent of a story about pop eating itself, but also frames the rich material within the context of classic noir heist movies. Her trademark, though, is anti-nostalgic remembrances of youth, full of bliss and pleasure, which are ultimately stopped in their tracks by time, politics, law, circumstance or death.

'For the filmmaker, war is probably the ultimate canvas.'

Kathryn Bigelow

B: 1951 / **N:** American

The Japanese filmmaker Kenji Mizoguchi and George Cukor of Hollywood's Golden Age are regarded as two of the greatest male directors of women. Kathryn Bigelow is the opposite: she is one of the great female directors of men. This is not to say that she is simply able to bring out the best in male actors (she is) – it's more that she tells male-centric stories, and is intrigued by what makes certain, adrenaline-juiced men function in society. *Point Break* (1991) smuggles an essay on jacked-up, combustible machismo into a story about bank robbers addicted to extreme sports, essentially positing high crime as the preserve of thrill seekers with shoulder-length, bleached-blonde hair and a knowledge of New Age philosophy. *The Hurt Locker* (2008) replaces surf and snow with modern urban warfare, suggesting that there is some obscure erotic pleasure to be gleaned from risking your life as a bomb disposal expert. Bigelow's is a cinema of fatalism, so it's unsurprising that she is most comfortable in the front seats of the theatre of war. Despite a notable skew towards male subjects, her films also offer us female protagonists with the attributes of men: take Jamie Lee Curtis's crop-haired, trigger-happy beat cop in 1990's *Blue Steel*, or Jessica Chastain's coldly driven, trouser-suited CIA analyst in 2012's *Zero Dark Thirty*. What makes Bigelow's films work so well is that she adopts the dynamism of her subjects and emulates it in the rhythm, pacing and lyricism of her storytelling approach.

The Hurt Locker, 2008

Touki Bouki, 1973

'I know that cinema must be reinvented, reinvented each time, and whoever ventures into cinema also has a share in its reinvention.'

Djibril Diop Mambéty

B: 1945 / **N:** Senegalese

At the age of 53, the Senegalese filmmaker Djibril Diop Mambéty died as a result of complications from lung cancer, at a time when many felt he had so much more to give as an artist. He lived by a creed of reinvention as a way to keep the artistic juices flowing. *Touki Bouki* (1973) is considered by many to be the greatest African film ever made, and there's certainly evidence for this argument. It opens on horrific footage of an abattoir in which cows are slaughtered and butchered by hand in less than sanitary conditions. We then cut to a young man riding a bike with a cow's skull attached to its handlebars. This is the story of an escape attempt – from drudgery, violence, colonial oppression, stifling tradition. From Africa. The man finds a woman to join him on his adventure, and Josephine Baker's 'Paris, Paris, Paris' is repeated on the soundtrack like a melodious siren's call. Mambéty pays homage to the formal tricks and playful tone of the French New Wave, but the romantic and stylized lens through which he captures the world is not enough to hide the trauma and degradation. Yet Mambéty's anger is always shrouded in humanist hope, and his films show the ugliness of poverty without ever blaming those it affects – a sentiment expressed beautifully in the 1999 short that became his untimely swansong: *The Little Girl Who Sold the Sun.*

'Cinema is a matter of what's in the frame and what's out.'

Martin Scorsese

B: 1942 / **N:** American

Who has the more interesting dreams? A regular, happy, carefree clock puncher, or an unrepentant sociopath? Martin Scorsese knows the answer and has dedicated much of his filmmaking career to tapping the unhinged psyches of some of cinema's most notorious (and charismatic) corrupters of morality. His famous quote above could be ascribed to something very specific and technical: that cinema is a matter of minute calculation and of deciding where the frame ends and reality begins. According to Scorsese, every frame of a film is the result of so many distinct variables – lights, shadows, angles, blocking, etc – that each and every one is like lightning in a bottle. But there's more to his comment than that, for it hints at one of the essential qualities that makes cinema a unique artform, and that's the choice of what we show and don't show in the telling of a tale. It's a question of articulation, elocution and grammar. I have chosen this image from 1982's *The King of Comedy* as sole representative of Scorsese's world-beating oeuvre. It shows us the life of an aspiring stand-up comedian played by Robert De Niro (in the frame) but declines to assure the viewer that what we're seeing is not in fact the protagonist's subjective fantasy (outside the frame). It is down to the viewer to decode the images and process the story as a kind of riddle, albeit a highly enjoyable one.

The King of Comedy, 1982

The General, 1926

'We build up a little story on some sure-fire idea, throw in a dozen gags, if we can think of 'em, and let 'er ride.'

Buster Keaton

B: 1895 / **N:** American

Buster Keaton stands here as representative of the creatively fecund era of silent film comedy, which encompasses many thousands of shorts and features. His long career was one of mixed fortunes, where a decade in which he punched out cinematic masterworks with alarming regularity (the 1920s) gave way to a twilight era of cameos, guest spots and roles in industrial short films. *The General* (1926) is a film that wears its life-or-death stunt work lightly; knowing there's no green screen net, it's sometimes hard to watch as Keaton films himself in a sinuous long take hopping along a moving train with all the grace of a ballet dancer en pointe. *Steamboat Bill, Jr.*, from 1928, is famous for a moment in which the edifice of a house topples over and Keaton is left standing in the space left by a window frame. An example of sense-defying stunt mastery, for sure, but also of total directorial precision, from the design of the sets and placing of the camera to the subtlety of the performance. Unlike fellow screen comedian Charlie Chaplin, Keaton seemed more interested in teasing the formal possibilities of this young medium, presenting his on-screen avatar as a symbol for this exploration, in contrast to Chaplin's Little Tramp, which offered us a figure of sickly empathy. *Sherlock Jr.*, from 1924, remains one of the finest examples of eye-popping camera trickery placed at the service of a compelling story, as a daffy film projectionist becomes trapped in one of his own projections.

'If it were all in the script, why make the film?'

Nicholas Ray

B: 1911 / **N:** American

The films of the Hollywood radical Nicholas Ray tend to feature characters either moving inexorably towards, or sullenly away from, a moment of violence. The director remains best known for his 1955 teenage angst psychodrama *Rebel Without a Cause*, a testosterone-fuelled chronicle of youthful insurgency and despair etched in crimson against the endless black of the Los Angeles night. Yet his CV is generously littered with outré masterworks that take timeworn genre templates and embroider them with quietly revolutionary details. There is no way you could read the script for 1954's expressionist western *Johnny Guitar* and envisage the visually florid melodrama that made its way to the screen, particularly that Sterling Hayden's title character plays second fiddle to Joan Crawford's plain-spoken bar owner, Vienna. The same goes for 1956's *Bigger Than Life*, in which James Mason's mild-mannered schoolteacher undergoes a wholesale psychological meltdown due to painkiller addiction – his descent into personal hell is visualized by low-angle lights that make it look as if our hero is wading through pools of fire. For Ray, the multisensory dimension of cinema isn't the only thing that separates it from typed words on a page. There's hard-bitten emotion too: take the happy-go-lucky sense of impending annihilation that pulses at the core of his roistering 1952 rodeo caper, *The Lusty Men*; or Robert Ryan's enraged city cop who is transferred to the snowbound climes of the countryside and saved by an untapped capacity for love in 1951's superlative *On Dangerous Ground*.

Rebel Without a Cause, 1955

Shanghai Express, 1932

'Shadow conceals – light reveals. To know what to reveal and what to conceal, and in what degrees to do this, is all there is to art.'

Josef von Sternberg

B: 1894 / **N:** Austrian

The expressive and emotionally energizing use of light and shadow is paramount to the films of émigré Hollywood director Josef von Sternberg. This is a hop and a skip away from the high-contrast, looming shadows of German Expressionism, for often it's the shades of grey that work the hardest. There's a certain understatement to Sternberg's quote above, with the word 'all' doing a lot of heavy lifting. His dreamy 1930 film *Morocco* takes full advantage of the cavernous souk in which the romantic clinch unfolds, as white-hot sunlight splinters through layers of exterior netting to create the effect of light being poured over his characters. It's as if they're being baptized. Von Sternberg's most formidable collaborator – and muse – was Marlene Dietrich, and he employed the landscape of her face as a canvas for his increasingly outlandish lighting schemes and camera set-ups. One of his greatest features is 1932's *Shanghai Express*, in which Dietrich plays Shanghai Lily, a woman of leisure who is riding a night train through revolutionary China along with a phalanx of unsavoury zealots, ineffectual fops and ex-lovers. Her precipitous moral journey – and how the other, self-consciously virtuous characters see her – is charted in the way she is enveloped by, and emerges from, a blanket of pitch-dark shadows. A famous sequence close to the film's climax sees Lily sauntering down a train carriage striped with thick shadows – the only character aware that the situation is in no way black and white.

'Filmmaking is an act of empathetic imagination.'

Isabel Sandoval

B: 1982 / **N:** Philippines

The cinema of Isabel Sandoval presents life as a compound of sensuality and crippling unease. She sculpts characters whose lives are dictated by the inexorable ebb and flow of political power structures. In 2019's *Lingua Franca*, Sandoval plays Olivia, an undocumented trans immigrant living in Brooklyn who works as a caregiver. She enters into a sexual relationship with her client's foolhardy son while doing her best to evade the authorities who seem, from every angle, to be closing in on her. Sandoval's cinema is pathfinding in its progressive depiction of trans characters, as they are more than the sum total of their sexual hang-ups and gender dysmorphia. Her films ask, how can we amply explore the sensuality of our souls and the nature of our identity when the walls are constantly closing in on us? In her remarkable debut feature, *Señorita* (2011) which was made in the Philippines, she plays a trans escort who, by a twist of fate, suddenly finds herself in the parochial world of local politics. Again, her character passes back and forth between two bisecting worlds: one of sexual danger; another of paranoia and small-town government conspiracies. Perhaps her pièce de résistance as a filmmaker, however, is an audacious sex scene in *Lingua Franca* which holds the camera firmly on Olivia's face as she experiences pleasure – according to Sandoval, an example of something elusive so far in the annals of cinema: the 'trans female gaze'. The sequence also suggests something utopian about sexual desire – the communion of bodies as the only respite we have from the dismal world outside.

Lingua Franca, 2019

ISABEL SANDOVAL

'I feel like the best films are essentially a Rorschach test.'

Señorita, 2011

You're interested in something you refer to as 'sensual cinema' – could you define what that is?

For me, sensual cinema is really about desire. And I think that's one of the main reasons why we go and watch films, or experience art. We are drawn to something that elicits that feeling of desire within us. The making of films is essentially a way for the creators or artist to project or translate the desire that they feel into something visible that can be experienced by spectators. I think it's also part of my personal evolution as both a person and an artist – especially after my transition. After my transition I've become more comfortable and more open about sensuousness and sensuality in my work, in that it's now no longer shrouded in a feeling of shame or guilt. I was born and raised a Catholic in the Philippines, and I think my transition and the psychological and emotional process that I went through helped me to overcome that. With desire, and tackling desire in art and on film, our experience with the art transcends rationality because desire is rooted in something more primordial, even biological. I would consider a film that I make to be successful if it allows viewers to experience desire beyond rationality. Where someone realizes they like or love a film, but can't pinpoint the reason why.

You are drawn to this idea of 'sensual cinema' in your own work, and in other people's work. Do you ever see films that you feel are the antithesis of 'sensual cinema'?

The antithesis of what I think of as 'sensual cinema' – and this is my personal take – are films that are specifically political, which I realize is a way of describing my films too, but I add sensuality to the mix. Some films are politically so specific that they don't allow any openness or ambiguity for people to project their own emotions onto them. I feel that some

of these films seem rigid and closed and don't allow audiences to engage with them on a deeper level beyond what they're purporting to say. 'It's about this issue. It's set in this country. It's set this year.' It is what it is. I feel like the best films are essentially a Rorschach test, and the more ambiguous they are, the richer they are because of that openness. I'm also of the thinking that our experience of art is never absolute or objective. It's always subjective – it means different things to different people.

'Sensual cinema' seems to be about people, bodies, bodies connecting, sex. It's quite a physical form of cinema, very people-focused.

For me, the most sensual films are actually about desire being repressed rather than being satisfied or consummated. I think that repression and actively yearning is a more realistic human experience than physical gratification. The films that give you the ending that you want and that sense of closure are energy expended. You can go back to your life and routines and everything is fine. But it's the ones that got away that linger within us. If Wong Kar-wai's *In the Mood for Love* [2000] ended happily, then no one would still be talking about it.

That's a film that has been key for you – even back when you were making *Señorita* in 2011, you cited it as an influence. What is your relationship with *In the Mood for Love*?

In the Mood for Love came out at a time when I was becoming more open and aware that filmmaking was my creative outlet. It's not a film you watch. It's a film you let wash over you. You experience it. You sit with it. It's a film that affected me beyond rationality. It's also interesting in that it's informed by some clashing impulses. It's about repressed desire, but the style and the aesthetic sensibility are so extravagant and rich and indulgent that you have a certain dissonance. And that appealed to me a lot. It's the same spirit that animates Douglas Sirk's work, particularly *All That Heaven Allows* [1955]. This idea has informed my work.

My take on your films is that you don't give much away in the form. In the acting, editing, cinematography, etc., you're not pushing the viewer in a certain direction.

Human beings are fundamentally inscrutable when it comes to our motivations and our psychology – why we do the things that we do. I think that's the main difference between my approach and more conventional screenwriting, because I feel like a lot of screenwriting is based on an assumption that the fundamental motivations are fixed or predictable. For me, I don't sometimes understand why I do certain things. Human behaviour is influenced more by the subconscious or subterranean than by what is immediately visible or obvious. It's in that blind spot that a film draws its complexity and power.

When you wrote your screenplays for *Señorita* and *Lingua Franca*, did you know you were going to act in the films as well? Were you writing dialogue for yourself and, if so, what was that like?

With certain projects, I know maybe halfway through writing it if it's something I'd also want to act in. It has to do with films that are truly personal to me, if not autobiographical. By personal, I mean it's not a studio commission or a studio project. These films tend to gravitate towards my pet themes, and it's something I didn't deliberately design but it's something I realized after making these three films that these are the films I inevitably gravitate towards, the main theme being women with secrets. And also characters who navigate two separate worlds. It's very obvious

in *Señorita* when she navigates between the quiet life in the provinces and her life in Manilla as an escort, and it's even more apparent in my upcoming film *Tropical Gothic* where a character inhabits two different worlds: one where she's a priestess, and the other where she pretends to convert to Catholicism to avoid persecution. These are kind of auteur-type films in that they almost write themselves. I realize that the protagonists in these stories are essentially alter egos. It makes sense for me to play them. But I also want to make the point that I only act in films that truly do feel personal. I don't necessarily want to act in other directors' work unless I really trust them. Also, I don't limit myself to writing or directing or editing. The works that feel closest to me, I want to give everything of myself to them. That's how I feel about my next feature too. I want to act in it.

With *Lingua Franca*, you were editor, writer, producer, star – the full auteur package. Is this something you want to keep doing in the future, to retain that level of artistic autonomy?

I want to go about it intuitively. And that's how I've gone about making my films to this point. That means I'm open to possibly delegating. Now I'm starting to get my foot in the door in Hollywood, there might be some projects where I'm being brought in for hire where I don't have as much creative control. And I'm open to that. I also hope I'm able to attach myself to projects that resonate with me. I think that if I ever did a studio film, I would then want to go back and make my personal films more experimental and adventurous.

A film like *Lingua Franca* might be deemed an autobiography in that you play someone who appears similar to yourself in real life. But that's not the case, right?

I consider *Lingua Franca* my transitional work. In a way I feel like the premise I was writing was the kind of thing that would get funding in the US. I also wanted to work on a piece that felt like it belonged to a certain genre – in this case, the social issue film. By working on a defined genre, I'm really able to subvert it. I can deviate from its conventions and its clichés to make the work feel unique. With *Lingua Franca*, I feel I married a political theme with something that's a bit delicate and lyrical. And I think that's what people respond to.

In all your films there is this link to the classical genre. In *Lingua Franca*, there is the more sensual and artistic side, but everything is couched in a paranoid thriller.

Before, I used to think that it was a deliberate creative choice. That I needed to contextualize these stories politically. Ultimately, I realize that I'm interested in power dynamics, specifically from the vantage point of a woman who is disadvantaged to some degree. The political milieu adds that texture. Politics is just the backdrop for the story in *Lingua Franca*. There's the pursuit of a kind of personal power within a system or a structure that deprives the character of that power. It's also about situating that power play within an intimate personal relationship between two people, and how that could be a microcosm for wider political inequalities. This is even more apparent in *Señorita*, and maybe more so still in *Tropical Gothic*. What I want to do with this new film is to define and flesh out the political context in the first half, and in the second I just want it to feel completely intimate and claustrophobic and personal.

The way you depict trans characters in your films feels quietly radical.

It's funny because I made *Lingua Franca* for myself; I wanted it to be something I'd be proud of. So I wasn't trying to make it for the broader cis gender audience. I feel like a lot of films that feature trans characters, even if they are made by queer or trans creators, are kind of like transgender 101. Or transgender for dummies. There's too much explanation for the benefit of a cis gender or straight audience, and I don't really care about that. That's not the kind of film I want to make.

In those films it's almost othering by proxy.

Exactly. So I wanted to make a trans character where there's an actual story and the plot is not about her being trans. I told her story without having to explain specific details of her life. There's an early scene where it appears that she's masturbating, but she's actually dilating, which is something that a lot of post-op trans women have to do. I also took the cue from a lot of the auteurs that I admire. They are telling the stories that they want to tell, and on their own terms. And they demand and expect their audience to meet them halfway and to rise to the level of the storytelling.

ISABEL SANDOVAL
A filmmaker who grew up and studied in the Philippines before moving to the US in the 2000s. She transitioned in 2014 and her films are delicate portraits of trans characters who, in the case of *Señorita* (2011) and *Lingua Franca* (2019), she also plays. Her second film, *Apparition* (2012), focused on a convent of Filipina nuns, and she has more recently made the short feature *Shangri-La* in collaboration with the fashion house Miu Miu.

'The main thing about directing is: photograph the people's eyes.'

John Ford

B: 1894 / **N:** American

The oft-quoted line about John Ford is that he self-identified as a maker of westerns – and with good reason. *Stagecoach* (1939), *My Darling Clementine* (1946) and *The Searchers* (1956) are among his greatest achievements as a director, and some of the most formidable examples of the western genre in film history. Yet Ford's interests stretched far off the reservation, and the term 'western' in this case doubles as a broad church for all manner of generic hybrids. Perhaps one element that ties his gigantic filmography together is a utilitarian style that makes room for great pictorial beauty (mainly the eerily expansive landscapes of Arizona's Monument Valley) and an abiding interest in the great themes (death, family, civilization, nationhood), while always ensuring they are baked into an efficiently ripping yarn. Where early Hollywood directors such as Howard Hawks, George Cukor and even Alfred Hitchcock had a keen sense of rhythm to the way they told stories, Ford had a sense of fluency, and remains one of the great, poetically terse visual communicators of the medium. There's an awe-striking purity to his filmmaking style, where the camera always seems to be in exactly the right place. It's rare to see a big or showy performance in a John Ford film – the famously inexpressive John Wayne was one of his key company members. This was a director who believed that audiences could pick up far more complex and ambiguous emotions if the actor wasn't transmitting them point-blank.

Morvern Callar, 2002

'Noticing and looking at things like a photographer, even when on set and everything seems already worked out, really helps me as a filmmaker.'

Lynne Ramsay

B: 1969 / **N:** British

The films of Lynne Ramsay derive from the mid-century British tradition of social realism, in that they tell low-key stories whose social intimations are far-reaching and intrinsically political. Yet Ramsay might also be seen as the product of the post-*Trainspotting* generation, editing with a certain pop dynamism, and filming with a precision that is sometimes coolly offhand (*Morvern Callar*, 2002) and sometimes more rigorous (*You Were Never Really Here*, 2017). She was rightly feted for her 1999 debut *Ratcatcher*, which seamlessly combined a squalid, documentary photography-like depiction of the 1973 dustmen's strike in Glasgow with the ethereal story of a young, poverty-stricken lad somehow finding solace and adventure in this dismal landscape. In both *Ratcatcher* and *Morvern Callar* there's a sense of urgency to the visuals, as if she's using the camera to needle and press for some kind of profound truth in her characters' lives. Yet there's also a sense of looseness to the way they are combined, which serves to make the stories feel combustible, reflective of the impulsive protagonists. With her later films, 2011's *We Need to Talk About Kevin* and *You Were Never Really Here*, that photographer's instinct evolves into something more stylized and elaborate, but is no less suited to the material she's adapting. Indeed, *We Need to Talk About Kevin*, a film about mothering and the banality of evil, is often made to feel like a series of tableaux from a fashion shoot, which in turn emphasizes the abstract nature of its central question of nature versus nurture.

'When you're editing, something happens that tells you this is the moment to cut. It's not theoretical, it's something I feel.'

Chantal Akerman

B: 1950 / **N:** Belgian

It would be disingenuous to compare the artistic impulses of Belgian director Chantal Akerman to those of a photographer. An off-hand version of landscape portraiture is occasionally seen in her films – take 1977's *News from Home*, which captures New York street scenes as the director intones letters from her doting mother. Akerman elides cliché in her shot choices and framings, and uses purposeful zooms and emotive pans to offer a sense of contemplative lethargy, or daydreaming.

This is at once one of the great New York movies and an illuminating text about the formulations of cities, the hidden codes in informal language and complexities of maternal love. Although her back catalogue is littered with superlative (if occasionally hard to see) features, shorts and installations, she is best known for her extraordinary 1975 film *Jeanne Dielman, 23, quai du commerce, 1080 Bruxelles,* about a working-class single mother who tends to various daily chores while moonlighting as a sex worker. The film, which merges radical feminism with the deceptive simplicity of a housewife's lot, redefines conventional notions of screen drama, insisting audiences engage intently with long, sometimes repetitive scenes for the near-imperceptible clues that foreshadow our heroine's downfall. One lengthy sequence involves Jeanne peeling potatoes and making schnitzel, while one major dramatic beat involves a button coming loose from her pinafore. Akerman occasionally toyed with mainstream formats (the musical in 1986's *Golden Eighties*; the romcom in 1996's *A Couch in New York*), but, as with all her films, these glossy experiments arrived with her own indelible signature.

News from Home, 1977

Three Times, 2005

'You need to spend a lot of time with your negatives, your raw footage, because then they'll talk to you and tell you how they like to be cut.'

Hou Hsiao-hsien

B: 1947 / **N:** Taiwanese

The depiction of time in film is vital to how a narrative unfolds. Done properly, it allows viewers to retain their bearings while navigating through the material. Even though they are gorgeously shot and ravishingly atmospheric, the films of Taiwanese master Hou Hsiao-hsien lean on the transportive qualities of long, fluid takes and the sudden transition between scenes. Hou sees an edit not as mere connective tissue, but as an ellipsis containing vital information that we are not party to, and that we must do our best to intuit. *A City of Sadness* (1989) can be a discombobulating experience, as it whisks us through the political to and fro of Taiwan's tumultuous postwar period with a minimum of contextual hand-holding. Yet the way it captures the rush of time passing, a feeling of invigoration and melancholy, is rooted in the workings of human memory. Hou is one of the central proponents of the Taiwanese New Wave and has been making mellifluous and expansive films for over 40 years. At the 2015 Cannes Film Festival, he won the award for Best Director for *The Assassin*, his inconspicuous but rhapsodic take on the *wuxia* (martial arts) genre, and his 1998 period drama *Flowers of Shanghai* is rightly described as one of the most beautiful of all time. *Three Times* (2005) is a romantic triptych in which the same actors play lovers in different times and places, offering a meditation, as the title subtly suggests, on how time itself distorts and discolours the exact same actions and dramas.

'One always speaks of films as if they were absolutes; yet we always see them in a particular circumstance, be it only because of the different projection conditions of each theatre.'

Jacques Rivette

B: 1928 / **N:** French

If David Lynch draws inspiration from his films by tapping his inner consciousness, the French director Jacques Rivette made films *about* that very process. His fascination with the enigmatic qualities of cinema, particularly the way it ensnares us within a collective fantasy (as opposed to a private one), was exemplified in 1974's *Celine and Julie Go Boating*, a meta-cinematic fable inspired by Lewis Carroll. To massively paraphrase this head-spinningly complex film, two female friends are magically transported from contemporary Paris of the 1970s to an old mansion house when they suck on a boiled sweet. In this house, a fusty mystery story plays out which they have the power to manipulate, revealing the film to be a madcap commentary on cinema's all-enveloping and dreamlike qualities, and our role as active inventors within this world. Many of Rivette's films boast a fantastical element which he leaves entirely to the imagination of the viewer. In 1981's *Le Pont du Nord*, two women traverse Paris on an obscure treasure hunt, all the while doing battle with imaginary spies and even a fire-breathing dragon. Rivette believed, in this instance, that you don't need to show a viewer something for them to be able to see it. Perhaps more than any other filmmaker in this volume, Rivette believed in the ability of his audience. By leaving so much negative space in his films, he was happy for them to fill in the blanks and almost become complicit in the production itself.

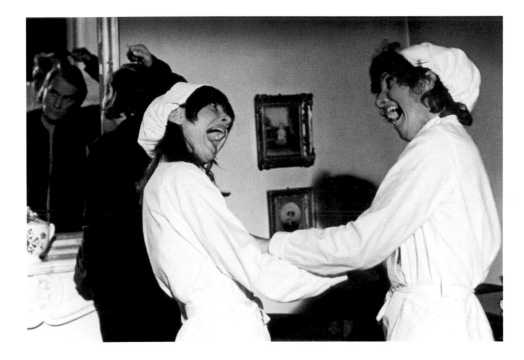

Celine and Julie Go Boating, 1974

Pickpocket, 1959

'There are so many things our eyes don't see. But the camera sees everything.'

Robert Bresson

B: 1901 / **N:** French

Aside from the fact that French filmmaker Robert Bresson produced an ungodly amount of cinematic masterworks (seven in *Sight & Sound*'s Top 250 films, published in 2012), he also wrote one of the greatest books about the process of filmmaking. *Notes on the Cinematographer* was originally published in 1975 and offers an index of pithy but vital epigrams concerning the thought patterns, deduction methods and intellectual minutiae that arise from making films. It also serves to unlock some of the filmmaker's more forbidding works, such as 1974's clattering Arthurian tone poem *Lancelot du Lac*, and his pitch-black essay on teenage nihilism, *The Devil, Probably*, from 1977. To return to that word 'process': so much of Bresson's methodology involved capturing the poetics of an ephemeral moment, such as a door opening, a bus moving, a prisoner going about his daily ablutions. His films often demonstrate a chronological obsession for showing how one action catalyses the next, how life is often the culmination of this continuum of humdrum processes. Everything the light touches he photographs with clear-eyed reverence, and every frame is pivotal to the construction of the film as a singular edifice. There's also a spiritual aspect to his films: his characters all seem to be drifting towards a moment of dark transcendence, be it the hapless thrill seeker in 1959's *Pickpocket* who puts too much faith in his right to personal freedom, or the donkey in 1966's *Au Hasard Balthazar* whose exploitation and torture mirrors Jesus's Journey to the Cross.

'The terrain of the face is the most dynamic thing you can point the camera at.'

Ava DuVernay

B: 1972 / **N:** American

It's hard to consider Ava DuVernay's 2014 film *Selma* without thinking about the relentless thud of marching boots. It is the sound of an inexorable march towards progress, an unbreakable rhythm that cannot and will not be interrupted. Her film tells of a peaceful protest staged by Martin Luther King Jr (David Oyelowo) in response to racially motivated violence and discrimination in the state of Alabama. A symbolic journey must be made between Selma and Montgomery, the sites of twin atrocities, and DuVernay stages this historical happening with a surface-level cool that barely masks the strident urgency of her all-too-prescient story. As a filmmaker, DuVernay displays a selflessness that is fitting of Dr King himself, in that, since the success of *Selma*, she has parlayed her considerable industry clout into amplifying an ethnically diverse range of voices through her ARRAY production and distribution outfit. Her abiding interest in America's dismal history of institutionalized Black oppression surfaced again in the 2016 documentary *13th*, which convincingly demonstrated how the prison industrial complex is an example of modern slavery, a practice supposedly outlawed by the 13th Amendment of the US Constitution. Even her intriguing 2018 children's fantasy film, *A Wrinkle in Time*, challenged tired Hollywood notions of screen representation by being centred on a Black teenage girl travelling through a fluorescent fantasia in search of her lost father. DuVernay is emblematic of the idea that every choice you make as a director is loaded with social relevance, even if you don't mean it to be.

Selma, 2014

Moonlight, 2016

'The history of camera emotion, 35 mm emotion, is racist. It just is.'

Barry Jenkins

B: 1979 / **N:** American

The systemic disadvantage suffered by people of colour working within the modern film industry goes back to the very chemical process used to develop celluloid negatives. According to Barry Jenkins, Hollywood made films for the eyes of white suburban audiences, so they had no need for Black bodies to appear authentic on screen. Jenkins' work offers an inherent corrective to this problem of representation, and his films, focusing primarily on the lives of Black characters, do so with a keen eye for colour temperature and aesthetic refinement. His aim is not strict documentary realism, but something more ethereal. Indeed, the people in his films come with an aura – a glow – of the type that the white stars of Hollywood's Golden Age received as a matter of course. His Academy Award-winning second feature, *Moonlight* (2016), seemed single-handedly to realign our expectations of how Black skin looks on screen, doing so even as it connected to a mainstream audience. The story, too, dealt with themes seldom discussed in films centring on Black communities, namely the homosexual awakening of a Floridian tearaway whose life is beset by a plethora of social ills. Jenkins' decision to adapt James Baldwin's novel *If Beale Street Could Talk* in 2018 felt like a perfect match, with his gorgeous rendering of this tragic tale advancing his belief that the creation of art is an inherently political act. The film at once subverts, critiques and celebrates Black culture, and does so with a lilting tenderness.

'A very simple image of what exists. That should be cinema.'

Pedro Costa

B: 1958 / **N:** Portuguese

Capturing a simple image of what exists sounds relatively easy. Yet what Portugese director Pedro Costa alludes to with the above comment is just how much the presence of a filmmaker can corrupt the sublime purity of reality, even if that reality has been lightly manipulated for the purposes of the camera. Filmmaking is the product of a multitude of decisions, but Costa tends to make those decisions based on a certain knowledge and understanding of his subjects – or perhaps it's more accurate to say a 'profound bond'. *In Vanda's Room* (2000) was the result of Costa embedding himself in a concrete maze called Fontainhas, situated on the outskirts of Lisbon. He leaves any self-conscious artistic 'baggage' (including a traditional film crew) at home, in an attempt to tell the story – or, at least, capture some inkling of truth – that is offered up by his surroundings. In this case, it's a moving portrait of a junkie who splutters and seethes in her room as heavy machinery tears down the surrounding buildings. He forcibly extricates himself as much as possible from the process, conscious of the notion that filmmaking is, by its very essence, an act of perversion and imposition. That such a humble approach to image-making could yield films of such power and aesthetic majesty is testament not only to the time Costa spends in deep contemplation, but the reality that only someone with such a rigorous sense of self-reflection could pan for the purest cinematic gold.

In Vanda's Room, 2000

AN INTERVIEW WITH
PEDRO COSTA

'Bringing cinema to the margins – it's a delicate operation.'

Do you find shooting a movie enjoyable?

It's a tricky question. I wouldn't want to speak for anyone else, but I have a feeling that the large majority of filmmakers would say no. It's terrifying. But, in the same way, and at the same time, it's a moment of such great tension and consciousness. You're very aware, or very open. It's a feverish moment. You're attentive to every detail. But you're also very aware of the fact that this is when everything will play out. Everything good or bad will be there in your frame, or in the eyes of your actor. In my case, it's quite particular because my shoots are very, very long. They're much longer than many of my colleagues'. *Vitalina Varela* [2019], for instance, took almost two years. I'm not shooting every day, but I'm there every day, talking to Vitalina, or helping Ventura [who plays a priest] arrange some papers, some bureaucratic stuff. That for me is also shooting. Keeping my mind occupied makes it more bearable. At the moment of shooting, you have to be really, really high. It's high tension levels. It's a bit like being in love, but all the time, which is not possible. It's unbearable, in fact! But you should be at that level all the time. The kind of fire you have to keep burning for a six- or seven-week shoot, is intense. We take one year, two years, and it means we can live the work a bit more. It's a little bit calmer. So in answer to your question, yes and no.

Casa de Lava, 1994

Is there a positive stigma to having a big camera on set for people to see, that becomes this, as you say, sacred focal point? So people know that a film is being made.

Again, I don't want to seem special, but in my case it's really particular. For *Vitalina*, I shot with the ARRI ALEXA, but it was the mini, a very small camera. When you put everything around it – the cables, the LCDs, the viewfinders – it becomes like a Christmas tree. I tend to use it very simply. Just the handle and the viewfinder. I don't want it too visible, but I don't want to hide it either. It's more in the eye of the beholder. Everyone who is shooting knows it's a very cold machine. ... It's a small box that is between us. ... Images are being recorded and stocked in this box, but the box is doing what we want it to do. I'm always in this double movement. I tend to protect cinema, in a way. I love it. I love the craft. I love narration, let's say – something that existed in classical cinema. On the other hand, I want to demystify cinema so that film is not charged with this special aura or romanticism. It can be romantic, but not that way. It's not something restricted to special people, the technicians and professionals and all those who know a lot.

You make the switch to digital after *Casa de Lava*, and go from a very big production to something very small and solitary. Was there a preference to shoot in this new way that strips back the classical notion of the big 'production'?

Yes, *Casa de Lava* was the biggest crew, lots of actors and non-actors. Shooting in Africa. Lots of trips. But every shoot comes with its own chaos. I'm not saying disorganization, I'm saying chaos in the frantic sense. If you take 80 technicians somewhere with some cameras and some lights, they will do a film and they can do it without a director. They will use a dummy, but the film will be made. It's a chaotic thing – headless and mindless in a way. I had seen it when I was assistant director, which I was doing for at least eight years. Before [directing] my first film I wondered whether making films was a bad decision. At that time I could say I hated shooting, but what I hated was the social system. What I saw was mimicry, an imitation of life. Every film was an imitation of the worst vices and schemes of our capitalistic society. At the time I thought, it's going to be a hard life for me and this is not what I want.

But I did one film, *Blood* [1989], and I tried to avoid [these problems] by bringing in all my friends from film school and lots of first-time actors, keeping it very amateur. My second film was *Casa de Lava* [1994] and it was a big jump. Producer, even some medium stars, French, a big crew, going around on planes, staying in hotels, etc. With *Casa de Lava*, because it was shot in Cape Verde, it was a miracle. I fell in love with the place, of course, but mostly the people. These were people who were not actors. They were giving their faces, their bodies, their feelings to me for free. There were some moments when I wanted to run away from [the film crew] and take the camera and just go and film some girls and dogs and children. And that's what I actually did a few times. In those moments, I thought maybe I wasn't made to direct actors. Maybe I wasn't made to be in this circus, and to always be ready and know what to frame. [On a subsequent trip to Fontaínhas, near Lisbon], I understood my problem was more existential: I had to organize myself better, in a more decent way. What I was seeing in films – and in my films even! – was a lot of indecency. Indecent things. Bad choices. Injustice. I had to take care of that.

You were seeing that in your films?

Yeah! I thought, if I can organize myself in this neighbourhood, a bit like in a studio in the old days, where I'm the boss, and I'll never be anything but the boss – I organize, I control, I frame, I direct. But maybe the gap between the wages that people receive can be much narrower. We can almost get the same, everybody. And I have to be careful of relations between people. Bringing cinema to the margins – it's a delicate operation. You cannot bring the trucks! You cannot bring the elephants ... I discovered that if the shooting is decent, and by that I mean more

transparent, that will probably contribute
to making your film more mysterious.
And I need that in a film. Films have to have
those mysteries, those intimacies.

**As someone who has spent many years
refining the process of filmmaking,
do you see any ways in which it could be
refined further?**

What I hate is this fake romanticism that
I was telling you about. When filmmakers
bring this aura to the creation of cinema,
it means that cinema moves out of our reach.
It's not human any more, it's very expensive
and it's made by very rich people. I hate that.
That's what I hate: rich people. I'm sorry. Rich
people and making films. No, I have nothing
against rich people in general, but rich
people making films – that's awful. Cinema
is very difficult to make, everybody will tell
you that, because it's very intimate. And to
keep it intimate, all the time, is a complete
paradox, because you're in front of a super
wide screen – or at least you were in the old
days – and you are watching very intimate
things. To keep the small things visible, but
also not to exaggerate, that's what's difficult.
But all the filmmakers who have filters and
special cameras are charlatans, who say it's a
craft, it's a certain way… No, it's not. It's just
being with people. There's a box between
you, but it's being with people. The pleasure
… is discovering people, discovering things in
people and how to work with these people.
If you have a decent relationship with the
world, the film will show it.

PEDRO COSTA
Studying at the Lisbon Theatre and
Film School under various luminaries of
Portuguese cinema, Pedro Costa worked
initially as an assistant director before
going on to write and direct his own films.
His sincere love of classic-era Hollywood
film grammar shone through in 1989's
Blood and 1994's *Casa de Lava*, and he
then started to make a more intimate and
egalitarian form of cinema, one of pure
empathy, with works such as *In Vanda's
Room* (2000), *Colossal Youth* (2006) and
Horse Money (2014), films in which he gives
himself over entirely to the life and world of
his subjects. His most recent film, *Vitalina
Varela* (2019), won the Golden Leopard at
the 2019 Locarno Film Festival.

'I'm not really a director. I'm a man who believes in the validity of a person's inner desires.'

John Cassavetes

B: 1929 / **N:** American

When you think about film acting, John Cassavetes should be the first name that comes to mind. He was an actor himself, a very good one too, often seen slumming in middle-grade genre fare for other directors so he could gather up the funds to write and direct his own passion projects. *Shadows* (1959) remains seminal in the way it beat the French Nouvelle Vague to the punch in its full-throated embrace of naturalism, and dismantles the romantic remove that commercial cinema had traded on for so long. *Shadows* is a jazz movie, about jazz musicians, but it also co-opts the structure and form of improvised jazz for unique dramatic ends. Many of Cassavetes' directorial projects starred his wife and muse Gena Rowlands, and her performances in films such as *A Woman Under the Influence* (1974), *Opening Night* (1977) and *Love Streams* (1984) count as some of the most extraordinary ever committed to celluloid. What makes these performances so extraordinary is that it is impossible to see where Rowlands ends and her characters begin, in part because Cassavetes couches them within a casually free-form framework that allows their power to be fully exposed. Consuming Cassavetes' work en masse leaves the feeling that – again, like a jazz player – he's constantly driving towards some skewed conception of melodic perfection. He achieved it with 1984's *Love Streams*, a film that seems shapeless and unwieldy at first, but then elicits its power by telling you that your first thoughts were correct – and that such is life.

'Each actor is a very different person, and each one has to be directed very differently.'

Pedro Almodóvar

B: 1949 / **N:** Spanish

Writer–director Pedro Almodóvar's initial muse was La Movida Madrileña – a punk/counterculture upsurge after the fall of the dictator General Franco in Spain – so it might seem strange to divert our gaze away from the florid formal elegance that is his trademark. Yet he's a filmmaker who doesn't receive his dues when it comes to the acting in his work, which is pitched somewhere between telenovela camp, Golden Age melodrama and high-serious theatrical. Beyond the luscious shades of fuchsia and red, or those divinely svelte camera movements, it's the performances that create a sense of cohesion in his mighty oeuvre. It's possible to draw a (non-straight) line from Carmen Maura's outrageous comic turn in 1980's trash opus *Pepi, Luci, Bom*, to the vapour-inducing heart-on-sleeve expressiveness of Adriana Ugarte in 2016's emotionally torrid Alice Munro adaptation, *Julietta*. The tenor of the films may be different, but the breathy romanticism and a slight ironic remove make them birds of a feather. *Volver* from 2006, meanwhile, offers the most complete and convincing survey of the quintessential Almodóvar performance, particularly in Penélope Cruz's Raimunda, a mother who becomes complicit in the murder of her husband when her daughter stabs him to fend off his sexual advances. She channels the full panoply of melodramatic emotions, switching on a dime between heated desolation, saucy humour and sincere melancholy. That Almodóvar is able to combine these divergent tonal notes to create harmony is just one marker of his obvious genius.

'One of the reasons why I make movies, part of the adventure that the process entails, is to make this kind of discovery of new souls, to put them before the camera.'

Joanna Hogg

B: 1960 / **N:** British

Since its earliest days, the movie star has been a valuable marketing asset for those in the business of selling dreams. Yet seeing these faces over and over, being made aware of a person's celebrity status, makes it more difficult for an audience member to fully suspend disbelief. British director Joanna Hogg has, across a small but impressive body of work, prized the thrill of the new, and has cast her films against the grain of name recognition. What she omits when acknowledging the pleasure she gleans from bringing new souls to the screen is that her films are all deeply personal and self-reflective — filmmaking as a concave mirror that offers a lightly warped but always discernible impression of messy reality. Her feature debut, 2007's *Unrelated*, presents itself as a satire on the elegant slumming of upper-middle-class English dandies, but is slowly revealed to be a painful rumination on the psychological effects of the menopause, seen largely in the awkwardly flirtatious relationship between timorous fortysomething Anna (Kathryn Worth) and braying posh boy Oakley (Tom Hiddleston, in his feature debut). It appears to be cinematic biography, though one fashioned from private impulses and interior reflection. *The Souvenir* (2019) is Hogg's most openly autobiographical film, and in this instance she counteracts the rawness of the memories as they come to her by casting her first major movie star, Tilda Swinton — though it's Swinton's real-life daughter who is the film's focal point and a proxy for the director herself.

Unrelated, 2007

35 Shots of Rum, 2008

'I make films with my weaknesses, my defects, my incoherences and my naiveties. I try to share things that nobody cares about.'

Claire Denis

B: 1946 / **N:** French

This is a telling quotation from one of the most sensual filmmakers to feature in this volume. It talks of subjectivity, and the feeling of crippling self-consciousness that comes from baring your soul in the name of art. But also the idea that Denis places a high cinematic value on desires and emotions from which other, lesser filmmakers might take great pains to swerve. It's a rare thing in movies: pain expressed with subtlety rather than hyperbole. At the heart of Denis' 2008 film *35 Shots of Rum*, Lionel, played by Alex Descas, hides his deep sadness behind a poker face, fearful that his social usefulness is coming to an end and that his daughter is looking to fly the nest. The scene depicted in this image is one of the director's most formidable, offering a shorthand for the subtleties of her style and reflecting her belief that information is better delivered by expression than dialogue. As the characters assemble in an after-hours bar, 'Nightshift' by the Commodores comes on to the stereo, and much emotional laundry is aired as dance partners are swapped and glances shared. Her interest in the dynamics of the human gaze is also revealed by 1999's *Beau Travail* in which members of the French Foreign Legion, stationed in Djibouti and sent out on endless training missions under the scorching sun, succumb to desires that professional duty demands they suppress. It's rare to fall in love with Claire Denis' characters, but we do take solace in their individuality and their ungovernable urges.

'As a filmmaker, you have to believe in the people – in their power – because if you do not believe in the people, then why do you make film... for what?'
Béla Tarr

B: 1955 / **N:** Hungarian

Hungarian writer–director Béla Tarr plays 45rpm genre film records at 33rpm speed. He uses cuts very sparingly, instead opting for sinuous sequence shots where his somnambulic camera slow-waltzes across, around and through a given space. Although Tarr's work may appear antithetical to the snappy 'genre' entertainments produced during Hollywood's Golden Age, he does co-opt the iconography and story structures of musicals, westerns and noirs, and then drags them into his own dismal microcosm of dive bars, boggy fields and desolate townships. *Damnation* (1987) is a classic film noir, but displaced to a run-down burg where the only true pleasure to be had is watching a torch singer at the local pub. It has the femme fatale, the tragic patsy, the scheme that goes wrong and the downer ending, but these elements are presented to emphasize the crushing duration of dead-end boredom. The artful expression of torpor, done in a way that is utterly compelling despite its testing duration, is Tarr's stock in trade, and the *ne plus ultra* of his project is 1994's seven-hour magnum opus *Sátántangó* (Satan's Tango). This includes a famous scene in which a young girl plays with a cat and becomes ever more aggressive with it. Tarr will not allow you to look away while the scene runs on and on. He pushes the idea that cinema has the ability to imprison you in a moment, and the director gets to decide the length of your sentence.

Damnation, 1987

'If we opened people up, we'd find landscapes.'

Agnès Varda

B: 1928 / **N:** French

When Agnès Varda uses the term 'landscapes' she's referring to beautiful but often inscrutable personal histories. People are mysterious, and opening them up reveals more mysteries, albeit of a more esoteric and expansive nature. Her 1985 film *Vagabond* stands as perhaps the defining example of this belief, concerning the final weeks of a young woman who is found dead in a ditch in southern France. The film is a psychological relief map of an unruly soul, and Varda yields dramatic riches from simply embracing intimacy and empathy. This vision of landscape can be read in a different way in her 1991 film *Jacquot de Nantes,* a documentary–fiction hybrid celebration of her husband, the filmmaker Jacques Demy, at the end of his life. His mottled, liver-spotted body is physically transformed into a craggy mountain range by the camera's tender gaze. Through her vast catalogue of features, shorts and installations, Varda casts herself as the intrepid traveller who knows that to walk these human ranges is to tap into something essential about human nature, and she did so from the first (with her quasi-ethnographic study of the French fishing village of Sète in 1955's *La Pointe Courte*) to the last (the affirmative public mural project *Faces Places*, from 2017). Varda was often seen as something of an eccentric, particularly in her later life, but it's a mischaracterization. She was a feminist, a poet and an artist who was earnest in her passions – and these passions just happened to include activism, literature, misshapen potatoes and cats.

'You don't make a movie, the movie makes you.'
Jean-Luc Godard

B: 1930 / **N:** French

You would need to pen multiple dense volumes of impenetrable analysis even to start capturing the essence of Jean-Luc Godard's drive as a film artist. Indeed, he plays a strong game in keeping that stuff hidden. Perhaps one route through his work is to explore a question of linguistics – of seeing the medium of film less as an artform, and more as a singular mode of communication. His seminal debut feature *Breathless* (1960) embodies an act of rebellion against what he and his intellectual cohorts saw as the existing movie industrial complex of cinema's first half-century. It is a film born out of counterintuitive creative measures: the cuts aren't in the right place; the lead is morally tainted; the sound is jarring; the presence of the director is felt through handheld camera movements. Everything Godard went on to do was at the service of militant (but provocative and judicious) iconoclasm. With each new film he refined this private, invented language into something that came in later years to resemble abstract poetry: works such as *Histoire(s) du Cinema* (1989–99) and *Goodbye to Language* (2014) are formidably obtuse. *Weekend* (1967) sits at the tail end of Godard's initial cycle of films, which contain trace elements of tainted DNA from cinema's 'glory days'. In terms of a desire for experimentation and a need to articulate ever more complex ideological and historical theories through sound and vision, *Weekend* can be chalked up as the lens of the looking glass.

Weekend, 1967

Goodbye First Love, 2011

'Making films is a way for me to harvest my own memories.'

Mia Hansen-Løve

B: 1981 / **N:** French

Autobiography tends to fillet the most dramatically pertinent events from any given timeline and place them at the forefront of a narrative. French director Mia Hansen-Løve does things a little differently. She somehow manages to see through the episodic minutiae of life and visualize grand emotional arcs that pivot around a single transformative moment. The way in which she unselfconsciously presents and frames the notable incidents of her own life with such candour and peculiar detail is moving in and of itself. And she does so in a way that recognizes the malformed and often ill-timed nature of life's high dramas, that personal histories can encompass the timespan of an existential awakening rather than just a bunch of interesting events. Two of her greatest works concern characters jack-knifed out of a state of idle comfort. *Goodbye First Love* (2011) appears initially to be a star-crossed teenage romance, until it's eventually revealed to be a film concerning the death of love and the slow grieving process that comes in the wake of that death. Then there's *Eden* (2014), which furtively charts the evolution of Euro house music in the 1990s as filtered through the life of the director's own brother. He spent his early years as an aspiring DJ until he reached a point where continuing in the profession he loved became impossible. An epiphany ensues. On that note, all of Hansen-Løve's philosophically rich films reflect on the affirmative or educational aspects of tragedy.

MIA HANSEN-LØVE

'For me, editing is ultimately part of what creates the soul of a film.'

The Father of My Children, 2009

Do you see any difference between a personal film and an autobiographical film?

Yes, if I look at other films, any film can be personal, and it doesn't have to be autobiographical to be personal. So of course I don't think my films are personal because they are autobiographical – I do see a difference. I'm so used to hearing that they are that I now no longer try to convince people that they're not. It's not that I'd like to hide it, or that I would like to pretend that they are not if they are, but it's just that I like to be precise. If I want to be precise, I would have to honestly say that they are not autobiographical because, if you look at each film, there's no film that actually tells a story that is literally about things that have happened in my life. If I chose to make a film about my life, it would be new to me.

The reason why people tell me this, or write about my films in this way, is because they can easily see parallels between my own life and the dimensions of the work on screen. And maybe it's because fewer and fewer films are written that way – and by that I mean openly using stuff that is inspired by reality and personal experience.

The reality is that not a lot of people know your personal biography, so everything is just idle speculation. The reason why people think that your films are autobiographical is down to the form and the way you make them feel like authentic memories.

Yeah, I think it has to do with what the films are, and not so much to do with the fact that they are literally autobiographical. As you say, yes, I do think it has to do with the atmosphere of the films and the fact that they somehow feel close to everyday life. There is nothing spectacular about them. And I think it's due to this lack of a spectacular dimension. There are no tricks in the scriptwriting. The stories are mostly linear. It's this that gives the illusion of autobiography. My work is always inspired by emotions and moments that have been important in my life. And the reason for that is I don't know how to do it any other way.

Prior to writing a screenplay, do you ever discuss ideas with other people?

Yes, I do talk with somebody. Usually, it's the person who's closest to me. I do need that dialogue. I don't think I ever wrote a film without talking to someone first and discussing what I would be writing about. I always need at least one person. There are some directors and scriptwriters who really need to bring in a lot of people and hear a lot of opinions. There are screenwriters who enjoy submitting their work to other screenwriters for feedback. It's a very professional manner of working. They talk very objectively about whether a script is good or bad. I have a very subjective and sentimental relationship to my scripts. Maybe I'm too fragile for all that. I do need somebody close to me to enter into a dialogue and help me gain self-confidence before I descend into the writing process. It has to be one person, maybe two, but never more than two.

Is that process about giving them something and asking for a response, or do you ask specific questions about their reaction?

It's very general. I would say I have an idea for a film. It's about a geography teacher who loses everything but ultimately she finds a way out without falling for a man. And then I'll say, I don't know but I think it's a really bad idea, what do you think? It often starts where I have something in my mind that I cannot get rid of, and I need the other person to help me have faith in this idea. They need to convince me that it's worth transforming into a film Not so much that it can find an audience. For me it's never really about whether this film can be a success. Not yet anyway. It's more about: does it make sense; do you think it's worth making a film about that; or is it an illusion? It's about self-confidence. I'm never completely sure about myself. I'm always in doubt. I feel very vulnerable to be honest. It's paradoxical because I can feel very strong and very vulnerable at the same time. My film *Bergman Island* [2021] deals with this idea. One of the reasons why I made this film was to try to understand this strange balance that defines my way of writing. This strange balance between self-confidence and vulnerability.

In the writing process, are you worried about structure? Your films always feel intuitive and flow in a way that never feels contrived, but is there a hidden structure underneath it all?

Well, thank you for saying because this really matters to me a lot. Actually, I don't like anything that has to do with conventional scriptwriting. I know my scripts don't follow the rules. When I started writing, that was more unconscious because I wasn't aware of the rules. I have never been to film school. I have never been told how to write a script. I had to develop my own rules. I started becoming aware when, after I did *The Father of My Children* [2009], a lot of people asked me to comment on the fact that the film was cut into two parts and that there was a shift as the main character dies in the middle, and then you move across to another main character. A lot of people thought that was very audacious. I started to reflect on that and analyse my own way of writing. But what I mean is, yes, it is very intuitive. What makes me want to make film is to try to capture a feeling of life. I want to capture life. That means I have to find my own mode of expression. I have to find my own language. I have to find my own rules. I know that you have very universal rules that just work and that have been proven and that we enjoy following them, and

I do think that, somehow, my films do also follow them. I don't pretend that the stories are written in a way where they completely sit outside of mainstream culture. I'm sure these rules are somehow there in my scripts and how I write them. I'm not trying to reinvent; I'm trying to react. That doesn't mean that I'm not working freely and not asking myself any questions – I do spend a lot of time on the architecture of scripts. I can spend months working on that before I write the script. I don't write scene, scene, scene. I want this storyline to reflect my own language, my own sensitivity.

I think your films express this idea that life is inherently dramatic, so you don't need to contrive it too much. At the same time, you're not making experimental films.

I don't like artifice. We see so much of that in films. I can't stand it, actually. It's part of the reason why I refuse all the scripts that are sent to me. Not that I have been sent so many. From time to time I receive proposals for scripts, and most of the time, after five pages – sometimes even less – I know that I cannot do it. I always feel the weight of convention, immediately. I lose any interest. It's not stimulating at all for me.

How has your relationship with your editor, Marion Monnier, developed over the years? She is someone you've worked with on every feature you've made.

We know each other so well, and we are very quick now in the way we work. We get quicker and quicker with each film. ... I have that [close relationship] also with three more people who I have worked with. Clémentine Schaeffer, who has been script supervisor on all of my films except one (because she was pregnant). I can't imagine not working with her. ... Even with my assistant, Marie Doller, who I've been working with since my second feature. And also Vincent Vatoux, who works on the sound in my films. As for Marion, we couldn't be closer in terms of artistic complicity, but on the other hand, she would never edit any film without me present. Since I started making films, I was always involved in the choice of every cut. I could never understand why filmmakers – and I'm talking about the ones who make personal or arthouse films – would choose not to be there in the editing. For me, editing is ultimately part of what creates the soul of a film. Deciding which take to use is so crucial. It's all the nuances that really define what the film is going to be. It's not that I don't trust her, but it's more about my own immersion in the film. I could not imagine doing takes on the set and telling the actors to be more like this or that, and then not deciding in the edit which take we should use. To me it's just absurd because when you are on the set, if you ask an actor to speak his line quicker or sadder, it's because you have an idea about the musicality of the scene.

You hear something, [so] it doesn't make sense if you have this idea, and then you don't follow through with it. I write my films, I film them, I edit them with my editor. It's the same music, it's the same movement, it's just different stages.

Can only you hear this music?

I think so because of where my films come from. Before I write, I go really deep into myself, or at least I try to. The source of my films is within me. It's in the past. It's inside some very intimate emotions. Each film starts with an interior music, or an image, or something that's invisible. It's something that's hard to define, but I have this thing in me that I will try to capture, develop and try to shape into a film. I'm the only person who has that. It doesn't mean that I don't need help and advice. I do need those other people, but in the end, I'm really the only one who knows what I'm looking for.

MIA HANSEN-LØVE
A Paris-based writer–director, whose work embraces a subtly poetic form of realism. Her 2007 debut feature, *All Is Forgiven*, revealed her fondness for unconventional dramatic structures, and she carried it across in films such as *The Father of My Children* (2009), *Goodbye First Love* (2011), *Eden* (2014) and *Things to Come* (2016), for which she won the Silver Bear at the Berlin Film Festival. Her most recent film, *Bergman Island* (2021), played in competition at the Cannes Film Festival, and she has nearly wrapped its follow-up, *One Fine Morning*.

'I dream for a living. Once a month the sky falls on my head, I come to, and I see another movie I want to make.'

Steven Spielberg

B: 1946 / **N:** American

Since his ruthlessly effective 1977 breakout *Jaws*, which alongside *Star Wars* helped to define the modern blockbuster, Steven Spielberg has always managed to galvanize both the deep-pocketed mainstream throngs and certain more rarified cinephiles. Certainly, there is a satisfying earnestness to such balletic sci-fi fantasias as *Close Encounters of the Third Kind* (1977) and *E.T. the Extra-Terrestrial* (1982), both of which have become touchstones for their symphonic sense-pummelling visualisations of cinematic awe. There is a dreamlike quality to his work too, but not necessarily in a structural sense; more that he drives towards a moment, or an epiphany, primed to leave the viewer in a state of ecstasy. His iconic presence within the industry means it's often forgotten that he is a master craftsman, particularly when it comes to the judicious melding of special effects and live action footage – see 1993's *Jurassic Park* in particular. The flying BMX sequence in *E.T.*, in which the alien helps a group of kids to spirit him away from government scientists, comprises the alchemically perfect combination of emotive composition, striking backlit colourization and John Williams' heart-tugging score. While retro-styled adventure films (the *Indiana Jones* saga) became an early trademark, some of his most interesting and radical work has been made since the year 2000: *A.I. Artificial Intelligence* (2001) is one of the most melancholy sci-fi movies ever made, while 2002's *Catch Me If You Can* underpinned that Spielbergian awe with a sense of crushing despair.

E.T. the Extra-Terrestrial, 1982

Escape from New York, 1981

'T me, films that e successful have s mething to do with l f and death.'

John Carpenter

B: 1948 / **N:** American

Film is inextricably linked with death because it's the only medium that allows an artist to depict, literally, that inescapable climax to the lives of each and every sentient being. John Carpenter's 1978 film *Halloween* etched a new set of rules when it came to the ways in which we process the often thrilling, sometimes nauseating, possibly upsetting spectacle of screen death. As a masked killer picks off teen high-schoolers in a sleepy suburban town, Carpenter foreshadows the monster's antics by making mischievous moral judgements about the targets, the simple calculus being that impurity equals death. One remarkable – and controversial – sequence in his second feature, *Assault on Precinct 13* (1976), involves a young girl purchasing a treat from a passing ice cream van, only to be insouciantly shot by a gang leader in the midst of a violent rampage. The scales of morality instantly tip in favour of the audience wanting to see this man receive his just deserts. In 1981's *Escape from New York*, death is omnipresent as Kurt Russell's one-eyed outlaw 'Snake' Plissken must, on pain of death, rescue the President of the United States whose plane has been grounded in Manhattan, which is now a city-wide prison fortress. The film's excitement and energy derive from Snake's refusal to fear this situation – instead we monitor his stony-faced long game to exact punishment on his bureaucratic taskmasters. Finally, in 1982's *The Thing*, about a violent alien who nests inside human bodies, death is inevitable, unavoidable and entertainingly gruesome.

'All my films are love stories.'

James Cameron

B: 1954 / **N:** American

In his two *Terminator* movies (1984 and 1991), James Cameron depicts a future in which self-aware technology has made a violent bid for societal dominance. And yet these cautionary tales have done little to deter this pathfinding filmmaker from recognizing technology as a vital aid to modern screen storytelling. And if the means to realize his outlandish visions don't exist, he will simply take to the toolshed and build them himself. Perhaps when he describes his films as 'love stories', he refers to his own love for the stories and the energy he channels into realizing them in the most formally consummate way possible. Describing films such as 1986's sci-fi western *Aliens* or 1989's deep sea ghost story *The Abyss* as 'modest' hits may seem strange, but Cameron went on to enjoy world-plundering successes to dwarf them both. *Titanic* (1997), about a love that couldn't quite transcend marine disaster, and 2009's *Avatar*, a sprawling eco-fable created with bespoke 3D cameras and software, became the twin commercial pinnacles of his career, both momentarily holding the crown of all-time box office haul. It's easy to take Cameron at his word that all of his films are love stories, as he is a director who ensures that any radical formal aspect is blasted into the mechanics of the story – making that hit of unalloyed awe all the more sparkling when it eventually arrives.

Terminator 2: Judgement Day, 1991

The Gospel According to
St Matthew, 1964

'The cinema was an explosion of my love for reality.'

Pier Paolo Pasolini

B: 1922 / **N:** Italian

The films of Italian polymath Pier Paolo Pasolini demonstrate that the term 'reality' can be subject to multiple definitions. The concept of his 1964 film *The Gospel According to St Matthew* was to present the life of Christ as terse realism rather than romantic fantasy. What if Jesus were a real person, and his miracles mere humdrum acts administered at random? Pasolini started out working in the neorealist vein popular in postwar Italy, and his 1961 debut feature, *Accattone*, remains one of the finest examples of this influential movement interested primarily in the life of the common man. His casting of non-professional actors and his fulsome embrace of life's squalid underbelly would remain with him until the last. All of his films, whether set in the past or adaptations of bawdy medieval stories (Bocaccio's *The Decameron*, Chaucer's *The Canterbury Tales*), speak to contemporary mores. He is a filmmaker with a thrilling sense of purpose and urgency. Prior to his brutal, unsolved murder in 1975, Pasolini directed *Salò, or the 120 Days of Sodom*, a loose adaptation of the eighteenth-century novel by the Marquis de Sade. It is one of the most punishing and difficult films ever made, detailing a procession of violent acts and sexual humiliation inflicted on a group of teenagers by four wealthy middle-aged men. *Salò* deals in the reality of degradation, as Pasolini remains unflinching in his belief that witnessing these horrors is the only way to truly comprehend the reality of fascism.

'Hollywood is exactly the same as it was. They still are not letting us in. And when you do go in, as everyone is magnetized to go in, you get white-washed.'

Cheryl Dunye

B: 1966 / **N:** Liberian–American

Justine is the name of the 1990 debut short feature by filmmaker Cheryl Dunye, and it contains the thematic DNA for all of her work up to and including her feature breakout – 1996's *The Watermelon Woman*. Dunye's radical film work explores Black sexuality, inter-racial relationships, depictions of sex and the insidious racism and class bias within lesbian social cliques. The director herself often appears on screen, usually addressing the camera and spinning a yarn that comes across as an erotically inclined diary entry. Her tone oscillates between the casually flip and the perpetually irritated, and we often see comic recreations of her words. A little like Spike Lee, Dunye articulates weighty ideas but both leavens and empowers them with humour and an intuitive feel for Black subcultures. While 1993's *The Potluck and the Passion* and 1995's *Greetings from Africa* are both dating comedies that pack a considerable political punch, *The Watermelon Woman* is revelatory in how it places all of Dunye's prior concerns in a historical context – in this case, the presence of a mysterious silent film actress who is credited as 'Watermelon Woman' and with whom the director, played by Dunye, becomes fixated. Her search for this enigmatic screen presence runs parallel to her romance with a white woman, and the film concludes that Black people – in art and life – exist only to appease the fragile, do-gooding egos of their white counterparts.

The Watermelon Woman, 1996

Waiting for Happiness, 2002

'I try to avoid making a show. Africa has been filmed in a showy manner so many times. Other people's suffering is not a show.'

Abderrahmane Sissako

B: 1961 / **N:** Mauritanian

The amazing director Abderrahmane Sissako understates the subtle poeticism of his filmmaking by saying that he opts to depict Africa in an 'unshowy' manner. He doesn't tell stories so much as allow the viewer to float through a moment in time, or to experience a situation that speaks of broader geopolitical machinations. His 2002 film *Waiting for Happiness* offers loose-leaf sketches of life in a tumbledown port town, where the prospect of upping sticks and finding a new life elsewhere holds daily appeal. Sissako views life as episodic rather than conventionally dramatic, and employs film as an illustrative medium for private quandaries, while also allowing us to project onto his carefree characters. In 2006's *Bamako*, Sissako elegantly diminishes the gulf between the political roots of African poverty and the lives of those in a simple housing block wanting to expose and punish the people responsible for their dire lot. It is a courtroom drama that takes place entirely in a ramshackle courtyard, and in the dock are the World Bank and the IMF. It works because the director does not lean too heavily on allegory, instead framing a piece of fantastical community theatre as an impassioned enquiry into a crime against humanity. The conversation continues in his 2014 film *Timbuktu*, in which the upshot of poverty is more than personal misery, it's religious fundamentalism. From Sissako we learn the vital lesson that it is not only possible, but sometimes preferable, to deal with the heaviest themes with the lightest touch.

'I think when you get all the money and all the freedom, rarely do you get a good movie out of it or a movie that you're proud of.'

Guillermo del Toro

B: 1964 / **N:** Mexican

The story of how Mexican director Guillermo del Toro painstakingly scraped together the finance and resources to make his famed 1993 debut feature *Cronos* has become the stuff of legend. It was a true test of creative mettle, one that eventually allowed him to follow a path that winds as much through a sunny upland of commercially viable genre fare as it does the shady undergrowth of his own baroque tastes and outré predilections. Who else could make a progressive parable about a mute woman falling in love with a humanoid amphibian and take home the Best Picture Oscar, as del Toro did in 2018 with *The Shape of Water*? The notion of limitation as the fuel for creativity is one that features heavily in this volume, particularly when it comes to filmmakers unwilling to muffle their own unique voice. Even when the cash is flowing more freely, del Toro delivers auteurist blockbusters such as his counterculture comic book *Hellboy* films or *Pacific Rim* (2013), about giant robots duking it out with city-levelling aliens and almost dance-like in its construction and choreography. Yet taking a more earthy, and perhaps more personal vantage, films such as *Pan's Labyrinth* (2006) and *The Devil's Backbone* (2001) include a mix of fantasy, sentimentalism and violence that lifts them above more conventional pretenders in the field. The images that del Toro presents are the product of immense consideration and do not exist merely to serve any preordained filmmaking etiquette.

Pan's Labyrinth, 2006

'Movies aren't finished, they're abandoned. And you have to make your peace with that.'

David Fincher

B: 1962 / **N:** American

Time is the enemy of the filmmaker. Resources are too. Unlike the lonely pursuits of writing, painting and photography, filmmaking (the version considered an industrial craft) is a collective art form where you have a narrow window to do what you need to do. As well as being a story about the unreliability of memory and the impossible search for finite truth in this world, David Fincher's 2007 film *Zodiac* expresses the idea that, sometimes, the work we do goes unfinished. As a technician, Fincher is known for his fastidiousness and the clarity of his vision, which definitely help when you're racing against the clock to ensure a set of workable images to edit. Following a successful formative career as a maker of music videos, Fincher was given his first bite of the Hollywood apple with the lucrative sci-fi property *Alien 3* (1992), which he famously disowned on completion. A cacophony of voices and influences (not to mention a barely existent screenplay) had made it impossible for him to realize his vision, so his abandonment of this film was forced rather than benignly accepted. It is ironic, though, that such a purveyor of cut-glass formal perfectionism would claim that what we're seeing are only impressionist sketches of completed films, when it's extremely tough to find fault with such pristine and self-reflexive titles as 2010's *The Social Network* or 2014's *Gone Girl*. Yet it's a bittersweet note on which to close: namely, that a filmmaker's work is never done.

FURTHER READING

Adair, Gilbert. *Flickers: A History of the Cinema in 100 Images* (Faber & Faber, 1995).

Bresson, Robert. *Notes on the Cinematographer* (Urizen Books, 1977).

Cousins, Mark. *The Story of Film* (Thunder's Mouth Press, 2004).

Hoberman, J. *Film After Film* (Verso, 2013).

Jones, Kent. *Physical Evidence: Selected Film Criticism* (Wesleyan University Press, 2007).

Kuhn, Annette. *Women's Pictures: Feminism and Cinema* (Verso, 1994).

Newland, Christina, ed. *She Found it at the Movies: Women Writers on Sex, Desire and Cinema* (Red Press, 2020).

Tarkovsky, Andrei. *Sculpting in Time* (The Bodley Head, 1986).

Thomson, David. *The New Biographical Dictionary of Film, 5th Edition* (Little Brown, 2010).

Truffaut, François. *Hitchcock/Truffaut* (Simon & Schuster, 1966).

QUOTATION SOURCE CREDITS

8 Jean Cocteau: *Esquire* magazine, February 1961; **11** Stanley Kubrick: https://scrapsfromtheloft.com/2019/11/06/stanley-kubrick-interview-joseph-gelmis/; **15** Lucrecia Martel: https://www.filmcomment.com/article/shadow-of-a-doubt-lucrecia-martel-interviewed/; **16** Ingmar Bergman: 'Ev'ry Time We Say Goodbye', *Sight & Sound* magazine, June 1991; **19** Abbas Kiarostami: https://www.youtube.com/watch?v=uSDWtdJKrG0; **20** Jane Campion: https://www.interviewmagazine.com/film/new-again-jane-campion; **23** Apichatpong Weerasethakul: https://www.theguardian.com/film/2010/nov/11/apichatpong-weerasethakul-director-uncle-boonmee-interview; **29** David Lynch: https://www.theguardian.com/film/2003/dec/10/davidlynch; **30** Rainer Werner Fassbinder: from *The Third Generation*, 1979; **34** Věra Chytilová: https://www.theguardian.com/film/2000/aug/11/culture.features2; **37** Satyajit Ray: https://www2.bfi.org.uk/news-opinion/sight-sound-magazine/features/satyajit-ray-moral-attitude; **38** Ousmane Sembène: https://www.youtube.com/watch?v=u9LP4nx-omnc; **41** Andrei Tarkovsky: Andrei Tarkovsky, *Sculpting in Time*, The Bodley Head, 1986, p.63; **42** Christine Molloy & Joe Lawlor: https://cineuropa.org/en/interview/108117/; **48** Werner Herzog: Paul Cronin, *Herzog on Herzog*, Faber & Faber, 2002, p.138; **51** Sofia Coppola: https://chud.com/7852/interview-sofia-coppola-marie-antoinette/; **52** Kathryn Bigelow: https://www.villagevoice.com/2009/06/24/interview-kathryn-bigelow-goes-where-the-action-is/; **55** Djibril Diop Mambéty: http://newsreel.org/articles/mambety.htm; **59** Buster Keaton: interview with Malcolm H. Oettinger, *Picture Play* magazine, March 1923 (transcript here: https://www.silentera.com/taylorology/issues/Taylor68.txt); **60** Nicholas Ray: David Thompson, *The Biographical Dictionary of Film, 5th Edition*, Little Brown, 2010; **63** Josef von Sternberg: John Baxter, *Von Sternberg*, University Press of Kentucky, 2010, p.18; **64** Isabel Sandoval: https://www.them.us/story/isabel-sandoval-lingua-franca-interview; **70** John Ford: 'Ford in Person' interview with Mark Haggard, 1970, *Focus on Film* 6 (Spring 1971); **73** Lynne Ramsay: http://www.bafta.org/film/features/the-journey-lynne-ramsay-interview; **74** Chantal Akerman: https://www.artforum.com/print/200404/in-her-own-time-an-interview-with-chantal-akerman-6572; **77** Hou Hsiao-hsien: efspublications.com/aninterviewwithhouhsiaohsien/; **78** Jacques Rivette: http://www.dvdbeaver.com/rivette/ok/daneyrivette-pt1.html; **81** Robert Bresson: https://scrapsfromtheloft.com/2017/08/22/encountering-robert-bresson-by-charles-thomas-samuels/; **82** Ava DuVernay: https://www.vulture.com/2016/09/ava-duvernay-directing-queen-sugar.html; **85** Barry Jenkins: https://believermag.com/an-interview-with-barry-jenkins/; **86** Pedro Costa: http://www.outsideintokyo.jp/e/interview/pedrocosta/03.html; **92** John Cassavetes: Ray Carney, *Cassavetes on Cassavetes*, Faber & Faber, 2001, p.159; **95** Pedro Almodóvar: https://www.theguardian.com/film/2006/aug/04/features; **96** Joanna Hogg: http://festivalcinesevilla.eu/en/news/10-quotes-know-filmmaker-moment; **99** Claire Denis: interview with Didier Castanet, *Journal of European Studies*, 2000, http://www.virginiabonner.com/courses/cms4320/readings/Beau%20Travail%20Denis%20interview.pdf; **100** Béla Tarr: https://www.indiewire.com/2019/10/bela-tarr-satantango-restoration-interview-1202182436/; **103** Agnès Varda: https://www.theguardian.com/film/2009/sep/24/agnes-varda-beaches-of-agnes; **107** Mia Hansen-Løve: https://lwlies.com/interviews/mia-hansen-love-eden/; **112** Steven Spielberg: http://www.scruffles.net/spielberg/articles/article-011.html; **115** John Carpenter: https://web.archive.org/web/20150228140340/http://www.theofficialjohncarpenter.com/pages/press/rollingstone790628.html; **116** James Cameron: https://web.archive.org/web/20171115203658/http://www.industrycentral.net/director_interviews/JC01.HTM; **119** Pier Paolo Pasolini: https://scrapsfromtheloft.com/2018/02/07/interview-pier-paolo-pasolini-oswald-stack/; **120** Cheryl Dunye: https://www.latimes.com/entertainment/movies/la-et-mn-cheryl-dunye-watermelon-woman-20161127-story.html; **123** Abderrahmane Sissako: http://africultures.com/interview-with-abderrahmane-sissako-by-olivier-barlet-5312/; **124** Guillermo del Toro: https://web.archive.org/web/20170702143344/http://www.moviesonline.ca/2014/10/guillermo-del-toro-interview-book-life/; **127** David Fincher: http://www.indiewire.com/2014/10/10-things-we-learned-about-david-fincher-and-gone-girl-at-film-independent-event-69212/

PICTURE CREDITS

9 G.R. Aldo/Films Andre Paulve/Kobal/Shutterstock; **10** Mgm/Stanley Kubrick Productions/Kobal/Shutterstock; **13** Mgm/Kobal/Shutterstock; **14** Aquafilms/Kobal/Shutterstock; **17** Snap/Shutterstock; **18** Nhk/Kobal/Shutterstock; **21** Jan Chapman Prods/Miramax/Kobal/Shutterstock; **22** Anna Sanders/Eddie Saeta/Gff/Kobal/Shutterstock; **24** Cnc/Tifa/Kobal/Shutterstock; **28** De Laurentiis/Kobal/Shutterstock; **31** Tango/Kobal/Shutterstock; **32** Paramount/Kobal/Shutterstock; **35** Filmove Studio Barrandov/Kobal/Shutterstock; **36** RD Bansal/Kobal/Shutterstock; **39** Films Domireew/Kobal/Shutterstock; **40** Mosfilm/Kobal/Shutterstock; **43** Desperate Optimists; **44** Desperate Optimists; **49** Moviestore/Shutterstock; **50** American Zoetrope/Kobal/Shutterstock; **53** First Light Prods/Kingsgatefilms/Kobal/Shutterstock; **54** Cinegrit/Studio Kankourama/Kobal/Shutterstock; **57** 20th Century Fox/Kobal/Shutterstock; **58** United Artists/Kobal/Shutterstock; **61** Warner Bros/Kobal/Shutterstock; **62** Don English/Paramount/Kobal/Shutterstock; **65** Isaac Banks; **66** Ruel Dahis Antipuesto; **71** 20th Century Fox/Kobal/Shutterstock; **72** Company/Kobal/Shutterstock; **75** Ina/Paradise/Unite Trois/Zdf/Kobal/Shutterstock; **76** Paradis/Kobal/Shutterstock; **79** Les Du Losange/Kobal/Shutterstock; **80** Lux Film/Kobal/Shutterstock; **83** Atsushi Nishijima/Paramount/Pathe/Harpo/Kobal/Shutterstock; **84** Shutterstock; **87** © Pedro Costa; **88** © Pedro Costa; **93** Lion Prods/El Deseo S A/Kobal/Shutterstock; **94** Avenue B/Kobal/Shutterstock; **97** Avenue B/Kobal/Shutterstock; **98** Wild Bunch/Kobal/Shutterstock; **101** Hungarian Film Institute/Kobal/Shutterstock; **102** © 1985 ciné-tamaris; **105** Copernic/Comacico/Lira/Ascot/Kobal/Shutterstock; **106** Les Pelleas/Razor Film Produktion/Arte Drance Cinema/Kobal/Shutterstock; **108** Les Pelleas/Kobal/Shutterstock; **113** Universal/Kobal/Shutterstock; **114** Avco Embassy/Kobal/Shutterstock; **117** StudioCanal/Shutterstock; **118** Arco/Lux/Kobal/Shutterstock; **121** Dancing Girl/Kobal/Shutterstock; **122** Duo/Arte France Cinema/Kobal/Shutterstock; **125** Tequila Gang/Wb/Kobal/Shutterstock; **126** United Archives GmbH/Alamy Stock Photo